The Book of LOVE NU

Find your ideal lover by understandi
between the special numbers of love.

By the same author
FORTUNE-TELLING BY TAROT CARDS
MOON SIGNS
THE LIVING HAND (with Malcolm Wright)

The Book of
LOVE
NUMBERS

Use Your Love Number to Discover Your Perfect Partner

by

David and Julia Line

THE AQUARIAN PRESS
Wellingborough, Northamptonshire

First published 1986

10   9   8   7   6   5   4   3   2

British Library Cataloguing in Publication Data

Line, David, 1946-
    The book of love numbers: use your love
    number to discover your perfect partner.
    1. Symbolism of numbers
    2. Interpersonal relations
    I. Title   II. Line, Julia
    133.3'35   BF1623.P9

ISBN 0-85030-473

The Aquarian Press is part of the Thorsons Publishing Group

Printed and bound in Great Britain

DEDICATION

To A.A.L. and L.L.L.

CONTENTS

CHAPTER ONE

An Introduction To Numerology

Your birthday — is it just a random set of numbers, or is there more to it than that? Numerologists say yes. They say that hidden meanings can be unearthed from the numbers which apply directly to you, that your character and your future is hidden in your personal number. And through a process of conversion from letters to numbers, even more detail can be discovered from your name, the name of those around you — even the name of your street.

Perhaps it's a hard pill to swallow, but just think how much numbers play a part in our everyday lives. Without them we couldn't develop the technologies we enjoy today, we couldn't measure dimensions and distances or determine how much something weighs — the list is almost endless. Just think how difficult it would be to sort one bus route from another without numbers.

The ancient art of numerology went hand in hand with the development of mathematics, geometry and trigonometry. Its roots can be traced to the early civilizations of Egypt, Babylon, Assyria, Greece and India and much of its core is based on ancient Hebrew calculations.

The element of chance comes into numerology — fortune-telling by numbers — as it does with most forms of divination. It is the nub of any divinatory doctrine and, essentially, the claim is that nothing happens by chance. All things conform to an inevitable pattern which we can do little to alter. So your birthdate, even your name, is not a random result from an almost infinite range of alternatives but part of a series of pre-ordained events which have little or nothing to do with luck.

In short, you, as an individual, a unique personality, could not have any other birthdate or name or have led any other course through life.

This belief can be taken to another stage — if you had a birthdate other than the one you have now, then you could not possibly be the same person, that special character, that you acknowledge as 'me'.

It is for these reasons that numerologists claim they can extract so much information from a mere set of figures. Those numbers are like a fingerprint and when combined with other details, that fingerprint — your personality and your future — cannot be mistaken for another's.

The history of numerology is complex and, as we have already said, its roots are to be found in many different cultures. Perhaps one man, more than any other, who contributed most to the foundations of numerology was the Greek mathematician Pythagoras who said 'all things can be expressed in numerical terms because all things are ultimately reducible to numbers'. The Pythagorean contribution was a method of interpreting numbers by qualities assigned to them.

But we must not forget another vital source which, with the Pythagorean philosophy, helped to create numerology. That was the Qabalistic Gematria — a belief based on the combination of magic and philosophy — which centered on the twenty-two letters of the Hebrew alphabet, and its corresponding numbers, to discover hidden meanings in the scriptures and to look at a person's destiny by name analysis.

Numerology isn't as complex as some would have you believe. The whole concept can be reduced to the numbers one to nine. Within these numbers the whole of life's experiences can be found. But you don't need special powers to unravel the mysteries . . . just simple arithmetic will provide the answers.

And what are the answers? They are virtually all you need to know to provide a guide to your future actions. Love Numbers, in particular, will help in the choice of a partner, or provide insight into how to adjust and respond to your existing partner. Numbers will also show you what lessons you are predestined to learn and how you can best achieve those goals. Taken a stage further, they will show you the vital directions for your career, indicate the sort of company which makes the best employer, or point towards the individual who stands out as an ideal business partner.

But don't confuse numerology with other forms of divination. Unlike Tarot cards, I Ching, Rune stones or casting dice, the study of numbers can give a complete and accurate picture of the inner you.

In this book we look at numbers in terms of your relationships, and the easy-to-follow guide will help you in your decisions. But if you want to explore numerology in even greater detail we suggest you take your studies further with *The Numerology Workbook,* published by The Aquarian Press.

CHAPTER TWO

Establishing Your Own Number

All you need to find your Love Number is your date of birth and some simple addition.

First make a note of your date of birth, remembering to show the month as a number — February = 2, July = 7, December = 12, and so on. It's also important to show the year in full, not just the last two numbers.

Now add all the numbers together, one by one, from left to right. November birthdates should be added as 1 + 1, not as + 11. Similarly, December birthdates should be added 1 + 2, and not as + 12.

If you have done your sums properly, you'll arrive at a two-figure number which needs to be further reduced, so that you end up with a single number between one and nine. This final figure is your 'Love Number'. A couple of sample calculations are given below.

Date of Birth — 29th September 1972
$2 + 9 + 9 + 1 + 9 + 7 + 2 = 39$ $3 + 9 = 12$ $1 + 2 = 3$ Love Number 3.
Date of Birth — 5th November 1955
$5 + 1 + 1 + 1 + 9 + 5 + 5 = 27$ $2 + 7 = 9$ Love Number 9.

Once you've found your Love Number you'll be surprised how much it can reveal about your personality. You are probably already well aware of your good points, and your shortcomings too, but did you know that your Love Number can help you to choose a suitable career or even influence the colours you select for your clothes and surroundings? Your Number can also help you answer some of those difficult questions that arise from time to time like 'What should I be doing with my life?', 'Why aren't I happy?' or 'Where did I go wrong?'. Not only can it provide you with the answers, it can offer valuable guidance about how to put matters right.

Each of us has a lesson to learn in this life, a particular path that we should tread, and your Love Number will point you in the right direction and help you reach your goal. But the most important aspect of Love Numbers is that they are vital if you wish to discover how well you are suited to friends, family and loved ones — or how well they are suited to you!

Each of the Numbers from one to nine has been given a bird, animal or insect as its symbol. This makes it easier for you to identify with your number.

Now it's time to find your Love Number and discover how much your number reveals about you and your 'inner self'. And once you've discovered what your number says . . . then it's time to look up other people in your life. Your search for the ideal companion can then begin.

ONE — The Leader

Symbol: The Stag.
Lesson: to overcome obstacles by personal creativity.
Path: originality, independence, concentration, confidence, perception, efficiency.
Goal: to express individuality and lead the way for others to follow.

Don't so much as whisper that something 'can't possibly be done' within earshot of a One, because he's sure to rise to the bait and, nine times out of ten, he'll prove you wrong — *he* can do it!

Ones are pioneers; they find the way for others to follow and succeed where lesser mortals fear to tread. Second fiddle just won't do for these powerful men and women; they will only be content when conducting the entire orchestra in a symphony of their own composition — and then not for long.

Most need no encouragement to spur them on and trying to give advice to a number One does about as much good as banging your head against a brick wall. If he's engrossed in some new venture, he probably hasn't even sensed your presence. However, should you manage to break through his concentration for a moment, and can persuade him to explain what he's so absorbed in, the audacity of his plans will probably leave you speechless.

Any criticism you may make of his ideas, no matter how sound or well-meaning, will only fall upon deaf ears. He does everything on a grand scale — the bigger, the more unusual and the more improbable the better. He is one person who can take a potentially disastrous situation, usually of his own making, and somehow emerge as the victor.

Once launched on a plan of action, Ones are powerhouses of energy. They work untiringly all day and most of the night. Sleep couldn't possibly be allowed to interfere with their efforts.

Ones can never be content until they have fought their way to the top in their chosen field and, once firmly seated in the boss's chair, they generally manage to keep their hard-won position of power and authority. They are usually much respected and admired by their staff for their sheer determination, if not actually loved. They keep a very tight rein on everything and everyone under their control, always knowing what needs to be done at any given moment and who best to do it, especially in a crisis when everyone else seems to be losing their heads.

These capable individuals take their responsibilities seriously, never side-stepping difficulties and *never* giving in when the going gets tough.

They work hard and expect the same from their subordinates — a half-hearted effort is one thing they simply won't tolerate.

When it comes to choosing a career, Ones should try to ensure that their innate creativity and originality can be used to the full — boring, routine jobs are not for them. They need plenty of opportunity for advancement as, without a challenge, they will soon lose interest and find themselves looking around for something more stimulating. The most obvious choices of career are as designers, inventors or engineers of one kind or another. Ones also like 'to boldly go where no man has gone before' but, unfortunately, openings for explorers are rather few and far between these days although some universities do offer research grants which might appeal to their sense of adventure.

From a negative viewpoint, One is traditionally known as the number of tyrants and people whose date of birth reduces to this number are quite capable of tyrannical behaviour when it comes to getting their own way — so be prepared for fireworks if you ever try to thwart the best laid plans of mice, men or number Ones! Stubbornness and an intense dislike of restraint are also firmly engrained in their character, along with impatience, intolerance and, occasionally, in later life, a tendency towards eccentric behaviour.

In private our monarchs of the glen need to love and be adored in return. There's no more pitiable a sight than a One who has been spurned. He'll probably say he's feeling under the weather or has something on his mind when really he's trying to hide his wounded pride. These people have tremendous egos and to be cast aside by their loves is more than they can bear; however, their natural resilience seldom allows them to remain downcast for long.

Once they have finally chosen a partner, usually after several traumatic false starts, Ones prove to be loyal, devoted spouses with a deep sense of responsibility for their partners and families. They are generous, caring and sincere in return for which they expect nothing less than admiration, flattery, appreciation and total obedience. They can be utterly ruthless if they so much as suspect their mate of infidelity and it goes without saying that they always have to have the last word in any argument. Ones of both sexes are charming, physically demonstrative and make exciting bed-fellows.

The female of the species is a liberated lady. She lives her life to the full and is seldom content to stay at home and keep house — she is ambitious and demands more from life than that. She needs excitement, luxury and pleasure because she's sophisticated, elegant, witty and certainly not modest. She knows that she deserves the very best . . . and somehow she'll get it.

She's certainly not afraid of rejection because once her sights are set on a man she is apt to take the initiative and ask him out to dinner, which on her salary she can easily afford to do.

These royal ladies, like their male counterparts, need to be the constant centre of attraction. Should her mate prove guilty of a moment's neglect or an inconsiderate action she will sulk and make his life a misery until her anger has abated. It takes a strong man to tame this lady but, once tamed, she'll remain his for life . . . and it won't be dull.

Colour plays an important role in our lives and Ones should go for gold as well as all the various shades of yellow (orange included), right through to the richest browns. To add contrast they could consider purples, blues and deep pinks but green, black and grey are definitely out as far as they are concerned. Their choice of gemstone should be limited to yellow stones such as citrine, topaz, amber and yellow diamond (to suit their rich tastes) with, naturally, a gold setting.

TWO — The Sensitive

Symbol: The Butterfly.
Lesson: to be able to 'give and take' when mixing with others.
Path: tact, diplomacy, gregarity, consideration, patience, pursuasion, friendliness.
Goal: to be able to work as a member of a team.

'I knew that was going to happen' said the Two modestly. But ask her how she knew and the only reply you'll get is an infuriating, enigmatic smile.

Twos have a highly developed early warning system all of their own; they seem to know from birth how to use their senses and instincts to attune themselves to their surroundings. You may not have noticed them because anonymity is second nature to a Two, but they have certainly noticed you and have probably already learned a great deal about you

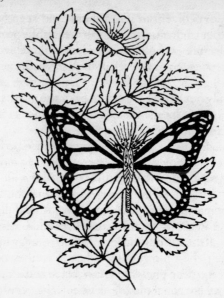

in their own quiet and unobtrusive way.

These shy, self-conscious people desire nothing more than a little peace and quiet, without too many ups and downs, so that they can go about their daily, well-ordered routine with the minimum of fuss and the maximum of efficiency. Not for them the star parts in a dramatic production. Twos prefer to play a supporting role on life's stage . . . the further from the footlights and the audience the better.

Quiet they may be but once you get to know them Twos are rather fascinating characters. But *you* will have to make the first move to get past that defensive barrier of self-consciousness so many of them seem to hide behind.

They have a surprisingly sharp-witted sense of humour all of their own which stems partly from their observation of people's habits and partly from their superb imaginations. Be warned, however, laugh at a Two and he or she will withdraw immediately into tight-lipped silence. They're easily wounded and take an age to recover from an ill-chosen remark.

Twos have an overpowering need to feel secure; they must have someone to lean on or something put by for a rainy day. At the best of times they're never really happy unless they think they have something to worry about but come the day that their security, whether financial or emotional, really looks seriously threatened they sink into moods of black depression which could even result in the need for medical help.

Twos seldom rise to positions of great authority in their chosen careers because they have neither the confidence nor the inclination to reach the top. They prefer, instead, to take orders from someone else and not to carry too many responsibilities on their shoulders.

They are conscientious, willing workers who, with just a little encouragement, will give much of themselves in return. A happy environment means a great deal to a Two and he'll only work well in peaceful surroundings. Pressure, deadlines and stress are definitely not for him; neither are decisions. Asking a Two to reach a decision is like asking a cat not to chase the birds — he simply can't do it. He can never make up his mind because he's always too afraid he will make the wrong choice.

People whose birthdates reduce to a two could get along well in most fields of endeavour because they never set their sights very high. Banking, insurance, accountancy and local government all offer ample opportunities for clerks, administrators, bookkeepers and so on — just the job for the unambitious Two. However, the imaginative, more sensitive Twos who are exceptionally gifted could possibly make fine artists, writers and musicians if only they can summon up sufficient courage to put their talents to the test.

Twos are sensitive and often suffer a great deal in their emotional lives, finding the early stages of a relationship particularly difficult to cope with, largely due to their lack of self-confidence. It's almost impossible for a Two to believe that someone can actually find him interesting or attractive. However, once safely past that agonizing initial period of getting to know one another, Twos can afford to relax a little and it is then that their true identity really begins to show itself.

Our male Two is an incorrigible romantic. He's tender, compassionate, a good listener and a considerate lover. He will do anything in his power to make his lady happy and will go to great lengths to avoid an argument. Once he has plucked up sufficient courage to tackle the responsibilities of marriage and family life — and this could take much time and soul-searching on his part — he should prove to be a loyal, caring partner and a devoted father.

Unfortunately he does have a darker side to his character which could cause problems in a relationship unless he learns to control his emotions. Jealousy could rear its ugly head at the slightest little thing and, unless you are prepared to constantly reassure him of your undying love and fidelity, he is quite likely to be moody and extremely irritable. His feelings of insecurity make him very trying at times.

Domesticity suits a female Two and it's a part she plays well; there's nothing she likes better than to run the home, arrange flowers or dinner parties to perfection and generally wait hand and foot upon her lord and master, with just one proviso — her efforts must be appreciated. Woe betide her poor tired husband if he returns home after a hard day's work and fails to notice the gleaming furniture or her new hairdo. Then the trouble starts — she'll retreat within her shell to sulk and won't come out for days.

A Two woman needs a strong man to rely on and if he can cope with her changeable moods she should make an excellent wife because a supporting role is what she needs.

The best colours for a Two to choose, for either clothes or furnishings, are cream, white and greens of all shades with perhaps an occasional splash of pale pink, to add contrast. They should never go for deep reds, purple or black because these colours are too positive and 'heavy' and would fail to complement them. White and cream are both neutral colours and would, therefore, maintain the anonymity that Twos are always seeking. When selecting jewellery, Two women should go for pearls, moonstones or jade, preferably in a silver setting.

THREE — The Versatile

Symbol: The Otter.
Lesson: to be able to express yourself freely.
Path: self-development, taking opportunities as they arise, convivial surroundings, working alone.
Goal: to achieve success and personal freedom through the development of your innate creative talents.

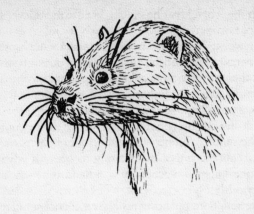

If you have ever been lucky enough to watch an otter at play you will know instantly why this charming creature has been chosen to represent the number three. He's bold and flashy, daring, brilliant, versatile and an incorrigible old show-off — in fact, he's a number Three with whiskers and a tail.

Threes, generally speaking, have a lot going for them; they just ooze talent, especially in the arts. They are those infuriating individuals who can dash off a masterpiece on the back of an old envelope while you're still experiencing great difficulties drawing matchstick men. However, despite his unnerving ability to do just about everything well, it's still very hard to actually dislike a Three; he has a certain charm about him which is almost impossible to resist.

It is small wonder that versatility is the keyword for this number. Who else but a Three could concentrate on more than one thing at a time? Threes have brilliant minds; they think at high speed and have the disconcerting knack of always being at least one jump ahead of everyone else. Their conversation is guaranteed to be both interesting and witty, if a little too direct at times. Threes believe in calling a spade a spade. They never mince words and in a battle of wits against a worthy adversary you won't need two guesses as to who will emerge the victor.

Occasionally they take a childish delight in playing a verbal game of cat and mouse with someone of slower mind. This may appear rather cruel but Threes are totally without malice and always let their 'mouse' escape with the feeling that he's really been rather clever for once.

Threes are born optimists who take life very much as it comes and adapt themselves accordingly. They are both lucky and happy-go-lucky, even an apparent stroke of bad luck will turn out to be a blessing in disguise for them when viewed in hindsight. If you threw a Three from a moving train he'd land unhurt *and* turn the incident to his advantage because Threes really do lead a charmed life.

Their faults are few, literally a handful, which can be counted on the fingers of one hand . . . thumb — wasteful, index finger — over-anxious for approval, middle finger — irritating to be with when not fully occupied, ring finger — sycophantic, little finger — unable to take anything seriously.

Threes are ambitious but never really have to choose a career because their innate skills have always pointed the way for them to go. Many reach university as a matter of course and so develop their undeniable talents even further. And it goes without saying that they gain their degrees with little effort much to the dismay of the slower students who find their studies demanding. While they are researching and revising, our brilliant number Three is probably relaxing playing rugby, rowing or organizing the forthcoming drama production.

'Otters' can be found in many walks of life — always well-organized and definitely in command of the situation but nevertheless always on the lookout for a chance to rise to even greater things. Authority suits them and they seldom experience trouble with subordinates because they are so charming to work for. They have the happy knack of getting the best out of people without appearing to be too demanding or unsympathetic to their needs.

When it comes to the most suitable career for a Three there are really two options open to them. For some the armed forces, especially the Navy, and government would make an excellent choice while others with a more creative flair might opt for a literary background or the performing arts. Journalist, musician, artist, entertainer — they can take their pick. Whatever the choice, the outcome will surely be the same — success, recognition and power.

In private Threes are not quite so organized and demanding as they are at work. They don't seem to feel the same need to be in complete control or to have everything running at maximum efficiency. Once they have entered into a steady relationship they like to share their leisure time and interests with their partner, and friends become less important to them than in their college days. Although this doesn't mean that our Three doesn't still enjoy showing off his partner at a party or that he stops getting involved in lively debates, he simply makes sure that his lady (and she's bound to be an exceptional person) is included in whatever is going on.

By and large Threes are not jealous people but they are quite capable of removing themselves from a situation which is not to their liking. They can stand so much and then, in a flash, they're gone without a second chance. But should you ever experience the love of a Three then your life will be more exciting, interesting and varied than ever before. What's more, he'll often surprise you with an unusual or unexpected little present to show he still cares.

Should you ever wonder, if you're involved with a lady whose birthdate reduces to a number three, whether it's your money she's interested in, the answer is a definite no. She is quite happy to enjoy it while it's there but if you lost everything tomorrow she would quickly adapt to the situation and would even quite enjoy the challenge of getting the most out of life for the least possible expenditure. This woman could turn poverty into an artform.

Most female Threes are outgoing women who like to have a career as well as a home to run. They like to be in beautiful surroundings although they can flourish quite happily in homes which are less than perfect. They like their men to be interesting, both physically and mentally, and soon tire of someone who is dull and undemonstrative. You don't need to be handsome but you do have to be on your toes to keep up with this lady and make her happy. Should you become set in your ways, watch out because she will soon seek more stimulating company elsewhere and she's sure to find it. There's a tell-tale sign to look for — she'll start nagging, nothing will be right. Then you must smarten yourself up or be prepared to lose her. However, she will probably tell you to your face what's wrong long before you reach this stage. She knows her mind and is quite capable of expressing her feelings in no mean terms. Stimulation is what this lady needs and she must find it in her relationship to be truly happy — all else takes second place.

The most appropriate colour choice for all number Threes is mauve.

This includes violet right through to the palest purples and lilac shades with blue, rose-pink and yellow providing good second options. Threes should avoid greens, greys, dark browns and particularly black as these colours do not vibrate well for them in their surroundings or in their choice of clothes. The best gemstone would be an amethyst as this is in tune with their colour mauve, with perhaps garnets to add some contrast. Both stones can be worn in any setting.

FOUR - The Builder

Symbol: The Bee.
Lesson: to be responsible for your actions.
Path: be prepared to work hard, pay attention to detail, don't take unnecessary risks, be patient, learn from your mistakes, be efficient, practise thrift, never give up but learn to accept reality.
Goal: to lay down solid foundations on which to build your life, to be practical and a good organizer.

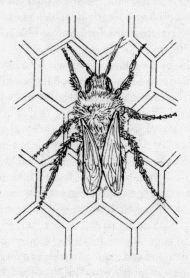

Next time you meet a number Four be sure to ask him what his favourite toy was as a child. It won't be the usual cuddly teddy, toy train or football

— it will be his construction set, whether it took the form of building bricks or something more sophisticated, and he'll smile happily as he remembers the hours of pleasure he had with it.

Fours are builders from the word go who need to know that what they create is based on firm foundations. They like life to be solid and dependable but they also like to know that they can expand, enlarge and develop, should they so desire, because the position they occupy is one of security and reliability.

Like their symbol, the bee, Fours are efficient, superbly well-organized and certainly not afraid of hard work even if, at times, it is dull and repetitious. They are practical, down-to-earth people who can be relied upon for their calm and steady approach to any problem, especially in times of crisis. Systemization is what they excel at and this is the main reason why they can get through an enormous workload with apparent ease.

But please don't dismiss our Fours as stodgy, boring people just because they are so industrious and precise in their work. Inside those solid, dependable exteriors lurk brilliant, inventive minds. They never appear to push themselves in company but somehow people seem to gravitate towards them in order to hear their amusing stories or to share in their jokes. Fours have the most infectious laughter and the innate ability to make others forget their problems for a while. They lead active and certainly interesting lives, with a generous helping of bizarre incidents thrown in for good measure. They're never at a loss for something unusual to recount — fate sees to that for them.

Fours have another side to their very distinct characters which, at first, may seem very much out of keeping with their practical approach to life and all its attendant problems. They simply cannot resist supporting a lost cause and more often than not they seem to take a perverse delight in viewing matters from a totally different angle to everyone else. Although they could never really be described as out-and-out rebels or trouble-makers, their desire to reverse everything and view it in a different light does tend to be annoying. In business life, their unusual viewpoints could make them a few potential enemies.

All the Love Numbers from one to nine have their negative as well as their positive traits and negative Fours do have a tendency to become gloomy when life isn't being too kind to them. However, their bouts of melancholy rarely last for long and are seldom bad enough to merit the description 'depression'. Surprisingly too, Fours are very sensitive individuals deep down, despite their practical natures. Their feelings can be easily hurt especially if someone close to them is over-critical or thoughtless. They also tend to be suspicious, rather than actually jealous, in their private lives. And they hate to think that something, however innocent, is going on without their prior knowledge and approval.

Success in business or commerce is rarely handed to a Four on a plate. It is something that they have to achieve slowly and usually only after a great deal of diligent work. Many start out in very junior positions and work their way steadily up through the ranks with managerial status often coming towards the end of their careers as the final accolade for all their years of effort and devotion to duty.

Money, although generally only the careful management of it rather than its actual control, often features prominently in their working lives because if there's one thing a Four can do better than anyone else it is balance the books. Absolute trustworthiness inspires a Four's employer to leave the accounts in his very capable hands.

Fours are gregarious and work well as part of a team provided that it is an organized and well-run unit. However, if things are in a muddle when they arrive, a Four will soon take charge and get things running smoothly in a matter of weeks. Committee work often appeals to them and many Fours can be found acting as unpaid treasurers or secretaries in their spare time just for the sheer pleasure of having yet another outlet for their organizational skills.

There are many career choices open to Fours of both sexes but the most suitable would be one of the following categories: builder, farmer, architect, executive, secretary, engineer, chemist, banker, accountant or even, perhaps, stage manager of a travelling theatre company. Who else could get a show on the road better than a Four?

Should you be lucky enough to have chosen Mr Four as your partner then you are indeed a woman to be envied. Life with him will never be dull because he's always bound to have some little surprise or treat in store. And he has much to share with the right person. He is kind, considerate, sensitive and home-loving, but he's one man who can offer you security without restrictions. Should you still want to see old friends or continue with outside interests he'll be the last person to try to stop you because Mr Four is a generous, big-hearted man. He would do anything in his power to make his lady happy. He would even forgive you if you spent all his money on a fur coat, and nobody is more careful with his money than a Four.

He likes his private life to be peaceful and trouble-free. In fact he'll go to great lengths to get along with his in-laws just to keep the peace. Quarrels and arguments are rarely caused by him. He sounds almost too good to be true; and he is, so long as you are prepared to return the love and consideration he shows to you. You must let him know where you are and what you're doing — he needs to be kept in the picture at all times or he'll worry.

If male Fours are the solid, reliable workers our females must surely be the queen bees. These women are capable of great depth of feeling. They prefer the men with whom they share their lives to be instantly in tune and sympathy with their moods. They need to feel loved and secure at all times and for this reason their homes are very important to them. Homes represent not only security but also something to organize and run to perfection. Monday is always washday for Mrs Four comes rain or shine — her routine must never be disrupted!

The lady Fours who seek interests outside their home generally opt for some sort of charitable work and if there's a lost cause or a lame dog around they'll rush to his support and organize help immediately. These women are loyal, faithful and supportive but sometimes too self-disciplined for their own good. What they need is to be a little less predictable and a little more mysterious if they want to keep the sparkle in their relationships. Reliability for them is a quality which can sometimes be taken for granted.

The best two colours for Fours are blue and grey including, strangely enough, the rather 'electric' tones of both of these. For secondary colour they can choose from fawn, pale green and pale yellow as all three are in tune with their particular vibration. However, they should try, if at all possible, to avoid bright strong colours of any sort as these will only have a negative effect on them and their surroundings. Their gemstone is the sapphire of any shade and in a setting of their choice.

FIVE — The Adventurer

Symbol: The Swallow.
Lesson: to discover the right way to use freedom.
Path: be progressive, keep up with new ideas and tackle problems with
    ingenuity, shun monotony and don't get bogged down, learn through
    travel and personal experience, use money wisely, experience as much
    as possible of life, seek variety.
Goal: to value freedom and realize that nothing in life is permanent.

Five is the central and probably the most exciting of all the Love Numbers.
People born under this vibration tend to view life as one long challenge.
They need to experience anything and everything that appeals to them
and are constantly searching for something new to try or somewhere
different to go. Like their symbol, the swallow, they need to be on the
move and seem to know, by some strange instinct, when it's time to
journey on and when to return to pick up from where they left off.

   Travel means a great deal to a Five, they simply have to know what's
going on around the next corner or over that hill. They are restless,
fidgety, impatient and born gamblers. They are always taking risks or
cutting corners, but fortunately they are both resilient and resourceful
by nature.

   Fives also seek their adventures on the mental as well as the physical
plane. They find a new idea to mull over just as stimulating as some new
place to explore. They like to be well-informed and to keep abreast of

what's going on in the world. These people are nobody's fools. You certainly won't find them getting involved in any hairbrained schemes just for the sake of a little novelty, they're far too realistic to fall into that sort of trap.

Adaptability is a quality that Fives possess in abundance. When life appears to have been less than kind to them they just seem to take it in their stride and quickly bounce back from even the heaviest blow. However, they are, by and large, rather highly-strung individuals who tend to live on their nerves and this is where they are particularly vulnerable. Once they have exhausted their reserves of nervous energy they have nothing left to fall back on and at such times their irritability makes them difficult people to get along with. But for the most part they are interesting, attractive characters, who are never short of company and always willing to lend a sympathetic ear or a word of friendly advice to someone in trouble.

Fives really don't have any major faults to overcome, instead their character flaws are small but numerous. They can be unpredictable which is irritating at times, a little inconsiderate when engrossed in something interesting, conceited when they feel they've done something clever and over-critical when you have. They're also rather careless with their own money because they love to speculate, whether on the Stock Exchange or at the local turf accountants. They are self-indulgent when their gamble has paid off but remorseful if they've lost.

Choosing the right career always poses something of a problem for a Five because they are attracted to so many different things none of which seem to hold their enthusiasm for long. They are also acutely aware that they could succeed at just about anything, they do so many things well, but deep down they're secretly afraid of failure. They have many self-doubts lurking in their minds although no one would ever suspect because they present such a capable, well-controlled face to the world.

Once finally ensconced in a job, for the time being anyway, Fives quickly show what a valuable asset they are to any employer. They are astute, creative and full of original ideas, easy to get along with although at times a little difficult to pin down. Restless they might be but they certainly know how to organize a team and have the knack of judging just when they can safely delegate some of their workload with the assurance that the task will be handled just as efficiently by someone else. In fact they are also very good at managing to pass on the more boring, mundane tasks without appearing to be shirking their own responsibilities.

Fives love to gamble, so the Stock Exchange is quite an attraction to them as indeed is brokerage of any kind because it involves that element of risk they seem to hanker for. Many are highly successful in commerce, medicine and the arts; the field of communications attracts others as does public relations and research work.

On a personal level five represents sexuality. In numerology it is known as the number of the natural man, the sensualist, and Fives of both sexes are certainly that. Even their symbol, the swallow, performs some unusual courtship aerobatics as it mates high on the wing. Mr Five may not actually require you to swing from the chandelier but any woman who has him as her lover is in for a rare treat or a nasty shock depending on her own upbringing and attitudes towards sex. But please don't let that put you off because he makes a considerate and affectionate partner, he's only jealous if given real cause to be and will usually only argue when provoked. However, should you manage to upset his normal poise he is capable of anything so don't trifle with his affections lightly. He won't tolerate that and will make sure you come off the worst in the long run.

He is not mean with money, he likes comfortable surroundings but doesn't mind a muddle and seldom falls out with his in-laws unless they interfere. Because of his masculine pride he does like to feel he's the boss in his own home and is never really comfortable if he feels beholden to someone, so don't go doing your Mr Five too many favours if you want to keep the relationship balanced.

Female Fives are real women who enjoy the role they play in life and live it to the full. Many don't marry until their early thirties as they need to spend the intervening years travelling the world and seeing as much as possible of different cultures and lifestyles. They know that they must get the wanderlust out of their systems before they can settle down and accept the responsibilities that a commitment like marriage will impose.

Once they've found a partner they put everything they have into the relationship to make it work. They take a great pride in their femininity, never plead a headache and enjoy raising a family. The role of wife and mother is a rewarding experience for them although they may not appear to be too keen on housework and cooking because they are routine tasks. Miss Five really can be treasure to any man lucky enough to marry her.

Fives should choose clothes and furnishings in very light shades of any colour and will find grey particularly complimentary to their character. They also look very good in white, as it shows off a tan to its best advantage, and anything shiny or that sparkles will bring out the best in them. They should avoid very dark or vivid colours as these will only detract from their appearance. They should also choose pale stones for their jewellery and diamonds are a must because they sparkle, with silver or platinum as the best settings.

SIX — The Peacemaker

Symbol: The Dove.
Lesson: to be responsible for members of your family and the community.
Path: be responsive to the social needs of others, show compassion and understanding, be loving and bring comfort, show sympathy when needed and try to equalize injustices through your own good judgement.
Goal: to be of service to others and give help and support when it is called for.

Ask a Six what he wants most out of life and he'll answer without a moment's hesitation 'Just a little peace and quiet'. That's the most important thing in the world for him and he'll work very hard to achieve it.

Sixes are also great homelovers with the emphasis falling heavily on family life. They make excellent parents because they are well-balanced and self-controlled, always ready to listen and always prepared to drop everything to help any member of their family who may need a little extra care and attention during a difficult stage in their development. Sixes are acutely aware of the responsibilities of parenthood and take them very seriously. They want their children to have every possible advantage in life and aids to education, particularly books, are one area they never neglect. In fact quite the reverse, their homes are usually full of books on a wide range of subjects. They believe that education doesn't stop when a person leaves school and that you're never too old to learn — a point they illustrate by being avid readers themselves.

All Sixes are creative and usually gifted in some field of artistic expression, especially where colour is concerned. They simply thrive in beautiful surroundings and they won't worry if their living space is small or cramped so long as it is aesthetically pleasing. Rich, vibrant colours attract them most, although these need to be broken up with carefully positioned, and indeed chosen, ornaments and pictures, which will quite often be those they have painted themselves. Sixes also have an innate desire to make people happy and often go out of their way to help others find a solution to their problems. Entertaining is also something they enjoy but the meal must be presented properly. Fish and chips out of newspaper, even if it is the arts review page, won't do for these perfectionists.

Sixes are usually successful in life and many find themselves in responsible positions relatively early in life. However, they seldom abuse their power and wield it with a wisdom and compassion which far exceeds their years. People closely involved with them respect their honesty and discretion, in fact many of their colleagues become close friends over the years.

Peace and quiet may be what a Six wants at heart but he can also be very determined when there's something he particularly wants to achieve and when angered, usually over a moral issue, he will brook no opposition. He must win! He likes to do everything for himself and although he wants to help others he dislikes being helped himself in any way. He won't delegate, finds its almost impossible to accept assistance, and is secretly afraid of becoming a burden to his loved ones in his old age. Money will never be of paramount importance to a Six but those who do manage to accumulate a tidy sum over the years often become patrons of the arts, if only in a modest way.

Careers for a Six tend to fall into two very distinct categories. On the one hand they could choose to follow a profession which provides a much-needed service to others such as nursing, welfare work, medicine, the ministry or marriage guidance counselling while on the other they could opt for something more in keeping with their artistic and creative needs. Many make brilliantly successful painters, sculptors, writers, musicians, teachers and interior designers. Whatever their choice Sixes should try to avoid a working environment which is in any way stressful or politically motivated as this would fail to meet their need for harmony and peace.

Our 'doves of peace' have a negative side to their character just like everyone else but, in their case, it tends to show as a form of selfishness. At times they can be over-dominant and try to force their opinions and views on other people. Occasionally, their desire to help others rebounds with the result that the person they were trying to aid becomes emotionally dependent upon them.

Sixes of both sexes are great romantics at heart and their love tends to be more chivalrous than sexual. Love for them is an ideal which should be treasured rather than a purely physical union which should be enjoyed. These are the people who write poems, send flowers, and dedicate songs to the object of their affections. They like to admire at a distance rather than come to grips with their passion. They are kind, loyal and always faithful to their partner both in mind and body. Their unyielding morality never permits even a harmless day-dream about someone else. Sixes expect fidelity in return for putting their loved ones on pedestals. If their sense of decency and honour should ever be outraged by an unsuspecting partner, you can be sure an emotionally charged scene will follow.

Female Sixes are motherly types who often prefer to stay at home and look after their families. They are born homemakers and devote almost all their waking hours to making sure that the house is just right. Everything around them must be pleasing to the eye and everyone must be happy. Only then do they feel fulfilled.

Colour is especially important to a Six and they should go for bright, bold colours, especially blues. All shades of pink and rosy reds are also very much in tune with them although they should keep away from black and dark purple. The gemstones for a Six are turquoise and emerald in a setting of their own choice; and it's sure to be the right one because they have a flair for knowing what goes best together.

SEVEN — The Mysterious

Symbol: The Owl.
Lesson: to develop the mind in order to gain wisdom and understanding.
Path: you must study, learn, search for truth, try to find the answers to life's problems; when you speak make sure you say something worth listening to; spend time on your own (this is essential for inner growth); study the past and the occult; read, think, meditate.
Goal: to be able to use your wisdom and knowledge to guide others.

Seven is the number of magic and mystery and those ruled by its vibration are indeed very special people. There's definitely something different about them. They won't act, dress, speak, think or even vaguely seem like anyone else you've ever met before — because they're not! These people are unusual characters in every way. They're unconventional, unpredictable and totally uncontrollable. They go their own sweet way through life without a thought for the consequences. They have to learn the hard way if it's going to make any impression on them at all. Sevens need to spend a great deal of time on their own in order to study, research, reflect and meditate upon the discoveries they have made. They seem compelled to try to explain the unexplainable and are sufficiently gifted to be able to combine theory and practice until they feel they have at least found some of the answers they were seeking.

Most Sevens will, at some time in their lives, feel irresistibly drawn towards the occult and all but a few will be found to possess powers of ESP or clairvoyance. Some will even experience remarkable dreams which they are able to interpret with uncanny accuracy both for themselves and others. Religion is also important to them but not in the conventionally accepted sense of the word. Money and physical comfort mean little to a Seven. They frequently dress in outmoded clothes, care little for their appearance and are inclined to skip meals or go without sleep when totally absorbed in some fascinating piece of research work or following an idea to its logical conclusion.

Sevens are independent and love to travel, taking only the barest necessities and just enough money to get by on. They don't mind roughing it, in fact that is what they prefer.

Negative Sevens run many risks, the greatest of which is losing touch with reality. If they don't keep a fairly tight rein on their highly developed imaginations they could find themselves being carried beyond the bounds of reality into a world peopled by dreams and fantasies from which they cannot escape. They could also find, because they spend so much time on their own, that it becomes increasingly difficult to form lasting relationships as they grow older, with loneliness as the only prospect.

Sevens need to choose a career with care. They have good ideas but seldom do anything about them. They also need to able to work at their own pace without deadlines to meet or strict schedules to adhere to.

The areas where a Seven could do well are: student, researcher, librarian, archaeologist, astrologer, inventor, scientist, psychiatrist, writer or anything directly connected with the arts such as painter, sculptor or musician. But whatever the course they finally decide to follow one thing is certain; sooner or later they are bound to adopt a philosophical attitude to life which will eventually creep into everything they do.

Sevens of both sexes are even-tempered, emotional and rather passionate. They have an intense dislike of heated arguments, preferring instead to discuss grievances calmly, sanely and unemotionally with the sincere desire to reach an amicable solution. Many marry well, more by luck than design, which is just as well because they need financial security to see them through life and somehow never quite manage to arrange it themselves. Marriage can also be just what they need to make them take a little more interest in reality.

Female Sevens are much the same as their male counterparts although rather more interested in the occult. Many women whose birthdates reduce to a Seven may be found working as mediums, clairvoyants, fortune-tellers and psychic investigators.

Gold is the colour for a Seven. Green and yellow are also complimentary as are any pale or pastel shades. Deep, dark colours should be avoided. There is a large selection of gemstones for number Sevens; any white stone is suitable as well as moonstone, cat's-eyes and moss agate.

EIGHT — The Materialist

Symbol: The Ant.
Lesson: to be materially successful and have authority.
Path: hard work, organization, sound judgement; use your energy
    constructively and work towards a specific goal; be ambitious; learn
    poise, assurance and self-control.
Goal: to demonstrate success and leadership by example.

Success is the name of the game that number Eights spend their entire lives playing. Not only must they succeed, they must also be seen to succeed. They seek power on the grand scale, money to surround themselves with luxury and, above all else, social position. All of them, without exception, are materialists.

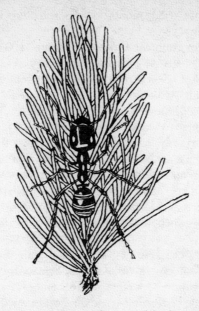

Eights generally realize very early on in life that you have to work very hard to get anywhere in this world. They're tough, practical, strong and tremendously ambitious. They work tirelessly and relentlessly towards their chosen goals with a zeal which almost borders on fanaticism.

Many Eights who make it to the top can be described as 'self-made men and women' because they tend to rely more on experience, their contacts and their own wit and cunning to achieve their ambitions. Eights can be hard and totally ruthless when necessary, never failing to take advantage of any opportunities for advancement.

Unfortunately, in numerology, Eight is not only the number of material success but also the number of material failure. It's all or nothing for our poor Eights — there can be no happy medium where they are concerned. Their failures are often just as spectacular as their achievements and when they do go down it's always in a very big way — but never for long.

From a negative viewpoint, Eights should guard against becoming over-aggressive and selfish in their unremitting struggle for distinction. They also run the risk of allowing money to become their god, having nothing but purely material values in life.

In a working environment, in which they spend 99 per cent of their time, Eights are imaginative, intense and driven by creative energy. They are totally reliable if not actually trustworthy — remember, they'll use anyone and anything to get one step ahead. They're also adaptable, self-disciplined and need little encouragement or support to get them started. They usually prefer to work unsupervised so that no one can really monitor what they're up to. Eights never have a smooth path to success but their determination and tenacity is usually all it takes to get them over most hurdles and set-backs they encounter on the way. What to do with their life is never a difficult choice for an Eight to make. They've never made a secret of the fact that they want to be top dog or that they admire and respect people who have managed to attain positions of power.

They have first-class business brains and many excel as bankers, brokers, lawyers and executives of one kind or another. But the mega-ambitious among them seek fame and recognition and for this reason are drawn to politics, government and public life even though such high positions invariably call for great personal sacrifice.

Eights are charming, attractive individuals but they do tend to put people off because, at first acquaintance, they seem rather cold and undemonstrative; almost as if they were trying to keep you at arm's length while they wonder what possible use they can make of you. But this isn't really true. They simply have difficulty in expressing their feelings and this can often be mistaken for disinterest but behind those stony expressions lurk warm hearts and passionate natures.

Unfortunately rampant jealousy also lurks just below the surface of number Eights. Many ruin potentially good relationships because of it. But, once married, Eights never shirk their family responsiblities. They'll do almost anything, and are prepared to make any sacrifice for their loved ones provided, of course, it doesn't interfere with business interests.

Eights like comfortable, luxurious houses but are inclined to be untidy. You're likely to find oddments of clothing and papers scattered around the elegant furniture. Their private life tends to be something of an emotional see-saw and they're either on an all-time high or plumbing the depths of despair. Somehow they can never quite reach the point where things remain balanced.

Female Eights need to have successful careers or they feel miserable and unfulfilled. Ideally they'd like to be able to earn sufficient money to employ a housekeeper, a gardener and a nanny to look after the children. They want the best of both worlds — a career, a family and a well-run home. These women know exactly what they want from life and invariably get it. They choose their partners with care as they couldn't possibly entertain any man unless he has as much money and influence as they have, if not more. They are mercenary and don't care who knows it.

The best colours for a number Eight are black, purple, very dark grey and deep blue. Brown and russet shades would also be complementary. They should avoid all pale colours without exception as well as bright red, yellow and green. They need a dark colour to give a striking effect. This should also be carried over into their choice of gemstones and they should opt for dull rubies, amethysts, black diamonds but perhaps, best of all, deep-toned sapphire. Platinum would undoubtedly be the best setting because it's the most expensive.

NINE — The Visionary

Symbol: The Badger.
Lesson: to develop a broadminded attitude to life.
Path: to be of service to others, show compassion and understanding; cultivate a working knowledge of world affairs; learn to live up to your ideals; be patient, don't give up half way through a project; do as you would be done by.
Goal: to show others the right way to live through your breadth of thinking and try to promote universal love and harmony.

Nine is the last and, perhaps, the greatest of all the Love Numbers, because it represents both spiritual and mental supremacy. All those whose birthdate reduces to this number have the innate desire to make some contribution, however small, towards improving life on earth. They want better conditions for everyone, higher standards of living and a fairer distribution of wealth. In fact quality and meaning are what they strive to put back into society.

Nines are visionaries, idealistic and able to see life from a broad point

of view. Their boundaries are infinite and all-embracing and they believe that everything and everyone, however humble or seemingly insignificant, is of importance and worth caring about.

Nines make charismatic leaders and extremely good organizers because they are resourceful, active, determined and courageous. They are quite prepared to fight for what they want, or for what they believe is right and frequently they have to do so especially during their formative years. Their strong wills and pugnacious attitudes are generally all that's needed to get them through even the most difficult periods of struggle and opposition.

But despite their genuine love of humanity, they have to be in complete control or their enthusiasm tends to wane and they give up completely until another good cause comes along that they can control. They also find criticism very hard to take because all Nines are egoists with very good opinions of themselves and of the caring work they undertake.

In numerology Nine is the mystical number. Many Nines, especially women, are gifted with powers of ESP which usually manifests itself in the form of telepathy and clairaudience. But in general terms these people are all highly imaginative and instinctive individuals who rely heavily upon their intuition, rather than on reason or logic, when problems need to be solved. Some also experience unpredictable flashes of insight into the future or disturbing prophetic dreams. The Love Number Nine also has its negative aspects and the greatest danger for those ruled by this vibration lies in being too impulsive in thought as well as in word and deed. They should also try not to be too overbearing, petty or prejudiced.

They are highly accident prone especially where fire and explosions are concerned, and few get through life with only the merest scratch to show for it.

Nines seldom have to decide what to do for a living because so many of them have personal vocations to follow. Many are destined for achievement although the path towards success is rarely smooth. They make inspiring and stimulating workmates capable of exerting great influence with apparently little visible pressure. But they can at times appear rather eccentric in their methods. Many become teachers, lecturers, doctors, statesmen, diplomats and politicians while the more artistically talented often turn to painting, sculpture, music or writing.

In private Nines are romantic, passionate and impulsive, always ready to try something new and often appearing with an un-birthday present or some little nonsense gift bought on the spur of the moment. They are charming, sympathetic and affectionate although when involved in some great scheme to revolutionize the world they can be a little insensitive to the needs of those closest to them.

Nines are passionate lovers, who always have some new fantasy to act out or idea to dream about. A personal relationship with a Nine is never dull and for those who lack stamina it can be an exhausting experience trying to keep up with them.

Nines value people and many keep in touch with their school friends for the rest of their lives. They love to argue but never seriously enough to damage their marriage and never with in-laws unless they interfere. They need to be respected and looked up to especially at home. A male Nine must be the head of the household and a female Nine likes to feel that she's the power behind the throne. Not only do they need to be respected, they also have a deep craving for love and a physical show of affection. For this reason many men of this number make complete fools of themselves if they fall into the hands of an unscrupulous woman who uses her physical attractions to manipulate them.

Within a permanent relationship such as marriage, Nines are warm and loyal, loving and caring, honest and trusting and only jealous or difficult when given good reason to be. They try to make their partner as happy as possible and to fall in with his/her wishes in most things.

They seem able to disagree without anger and to reach a working compromise with a certain degree of humour. All in all they are easy to get along with.

Female Nines are much the same as their male counterparts. They too possess a sincere wish to help others and many successfully manage to combine this with the demands that a home and family impose upon them.

Pink is the most suitable choice of colour for a Nine right through rose, crimson, red and purple to the darkest shade of mauve. The richer the colour the better. All shades of blue are also in tune with this number although greens, yellows, browns and black should be avoided. With gemstones, rubies, garnets or bloodstones would all do well in any type of setting which appeals to the individual.

CHAPTER THREE

Find Your Ideal Partner

Male One:Female One

Compromise and co-operation are called for when two Ones decide to join forces in a relationship, unless they both want to spend all their time playing a never-ending game of one-upmanship.

Mr One has met his match with this lady. Intellectually she is his double with an outlook on life almost identical to his own. She's stubborn, impatient, ambitious, hard-working and, what's more, she has feminine charm on her side which she won't think twice about exploiting to gain a little extra ground. This pair is really going to have to work hard to keep the combination together. They should always try to avoid putting themselves in competitive situations; even more difficult should they work as well as live together. In such a case it's anyone's guess who will emerge the victor.

Secondly, in a 1:1 combination, Mr One can forget that rosy picture he likes to imagine of the little woman sitting at home with his slippers warming by the fire for him to slip into when he returns tired and hungry after a hard day's work. Miss One will probably have a similarly high-powered, prestigious job of her own so they'll undoubtedly find it necessary to divide the household chores equally between them. In fact they may not see a great deal of each other except at weekends because they'll both be busy pursuing their own careers and neither will have that much time to spend at home watching television or just dozing in a comfortable arm-chair.

Miss One should really make sure that she knows what she's letting herself in for before she decides to tackle a male of her own number type. He is probably one of the few men who know how to play her at their own game and he knows that there aren't any rules, so she certainly won't be able to push him around as she does everyone else. She'll certainly have to make a few major adjustments to her 'me first' attitude if she ever hopes to co-exist on equal terms for longer than a few weeks with this man. She will have to learn to use the term 'we' more often than 'I' and be prepared to share the stage when she has Mr One for a partner. No more solo performances for her. It will have to be a double act or the show simply won't go on.

As well as fixed ideas, male Ones also have massive egos so, if at all possible, she should try to appear a little more helpless and more dependent upon him than she actually is, just to satisfy his male vanity. She knows full well that there is nothing he can do that she couldn't do equally well, if not better, but a little flattery and a mock show of submissiveness from time to time will go a long way to smoothing the path of this relationship.

However, behind locked doors — bedroom or otherwise — the intimate side of their relationship is guaranteed to be the most exciting of all because they're both passionate, demonstrative and inventive by nature so there shouldn't ever be any real reason for either of them to complain. Miss One won't be prepared to take a passive role all the time. She's a woman who needs equality and, even under covers, the 'give and take' that they will both need to work hard to achieve must never be allowed to slip.

Ones usually remain loyal and devoted provided they feel happy and fulfilled within a relationship, so if the male is prepared to make the effort not to be too domineering and his partner is ready to meet him half-way he won't need to worry over-much about his Number One woman seeking her pleasures elsewhere. Nor she about him! This relationship can really work and has great potential provided both partners are equally determined to make it a joint success.

Male One:Female Two

Miss Two is the very lady that Mr One has been waiting for. When he finds her he should never let her go. She may not be as dynamic as some of the women he competes against; she may not cause a stir, or even the odd couple of heads to turn, when she enters a room, but at least he can feel completely at his ease with her. Even Mr One, who is rather inclined to burn the midnight oil when he's engaged in some particularly fascinating piece of work, needs to relax occasionally. He can't go driving himself flat out all the time. What's more this woman would never question his right to be head of the household because that's the role she would automatically expect him to assume. She would be only too willing to help him in any way she could, she'd never interrupt when he was trying to concentrate and would worship the ground he trod on.

Miss Two has much to contribute to this relationship. She is quiet, admittedly, but then he's quite capable of making enough noise for the pair of them so that wouldn't matter. But behind her passive exterior lurks a wicked sense of humour. She has a wonderful imagination and the uncanny knack of being able to sum up a person at first sight. Mr One could find this extremely useful at times when he needs a quick, accurate character assessment of someone he's been trying to weigh up.

Unfortunately, Miss Two lacks confidence and often asks herself rather self-effacingly: 'I wonder what he sees in me because really I don't think I'm in the least bit interesting or attractive'. And the answer is, quite simply 'everything'; he's drawn to her because opposites attract. He can't understand why she is not ambitious (although he's secretly glad she's not), he wants to know exactly what is going on inside that head of hers because she doesn't give much away but, above all, she's a good listener and that's something he positively approves of.

She, in turn, admires him because he represents everything that she is not. He has already decided what he wants from life, he's not afraid of responsibility, has plenty to say for himself and is so positive about everything. He is someone she can lean on and all Twos are rather inclined to do that from time to time.

Mr One will have to treat this lady gently because she's not nearly as thick-skinned as he is. She needs to feel secure and protected at all times; she is easily hurt and her efforts on his behalf must always be appreciated. A little praise will make her smile and with encouragement she could become positively radiant. She needs a strong man to depend upon and Mr One fits the bill exactly.

In return she will run his home like clockwork, wait upon him hand and foot, raise their children with loving care and entertain his business associates like the born hostess she is. However, they could find, in this particular relationship, that problems arise if he has to be away on business a good deal or if his job entails working long, irregular hours. Miss Two is a homelover, she probably won't have many outside interests and will want to spend her evenings and weekends exclusively with her man which may not always be possible. Then her sulky and changeable moods could be rather difficult for him to endure. She's also incurably jealous of anything which is likely to deprive her of his company.

In private he can expect to receive royal treatment and to be shown nothing less than adoration from this woman. She will look up to him, flatter him, do as she's told, be loyal — in fact she'll be totally besotted with him. And all this is just what he needs because, if he's truthful, he's always been a bit of a male chauvinist at heart who believes that a woman's place is in the home.

Female Twos are incurable romantics. They are tender and loving, affectionate and kind while their partner is the more aggressive, demonstrative type which is just as well because he'll probably have to take the initiative in their lovemaking, although she will always respond eagerly to his suggestions. She is an introverted person and likes to assume the safe, passive role in everything she does. She is terribly unsure of herself but finds his advances exciting and somehow rather reassuring because they prove that he still finds her attractive. But deep down she has always known that she can really let herself go with Mr One and she may dream up a few fantasies from the vivid imagination of hers that would surprise even him.

Male One:Female Three

You won't have to ask Mr One what he sees in Miss Three because anyone can tell at a glance what the attraction is — she's a charming, fascinating woman who would stand out immediately in any crowd. And she's not just physically attractive, with her dramatic hair-style and bold choice of unusual but stylish clothes — this woman also has brains. She is shrewd, observant, imaginative and has the infuriating habit of appearing to be one step ahead of everyone else's train of thought — which Mr One finds rather challenging. She's proud, independent and very much to the point when she has one to make. She has every intention of doing extremely well for herself but in the meantime she's going to enjoy life to the full.

Once off duty, which isn't very often in Mr One's case, he is a fun person to have around provided that everyone else falls in with his plans — he has to lead the way even during leisure time. However, because he always seems to suggest such unusual, exciting things to do his ideas rarely meet with opposition, especially not from Miss Three. She is versatile, adaptable and game for anything. She loves to be in beautiful surroundings but would willingly leave her comfortable little flat to live in a tent if the right man asked her to share it with him. And Mr One is quite likely to make such a request although canvas and sleeping bags would probably only be a holiday arrangement.

Miss Three is a talented woman; she is artistic and creative and would soon leave her mark on any home they decided to share. The best choice of colours for a Three are purples and mauves which are both secondary colours for a One so they shouldn't argue too much over the way their home is decorated and furnished.

Mr One has a deep sense of responsibility for those he loves and this particular woman could be quite a handful for him. He is rarely extravagant but if she was feeling particularly generous one week she could well decide to spend all the housekeeping on presents for him and their family. He probably wouldn't make too much fuss provided it didn't happen too often but should her impulsive spending get out of hand he could turn very nasty indeed. Ones seldom look for arguments but you can be sure that they always end up having the last word to say on any subject.

Miss Three can also be wasteful and rather frivolous at times so if she fails to take any of his ideas seriously, especially if they are in connection with his job, he could find her 'silly' attitude particularly infuriating.

Mr One makes an exciting bedfellow for any responsive, red-blooded woman because he's charming, demonstrative, passionate and, at times, downright aggressive in his approach to lovemaking. He's not a man to fool around, he wants adventure even in his private life so any woman who tends to suffer from headaches is not his type. But Miss Three certainly is, she always has a very clear head. She likes variety and soon tires of dull, uninteresting men who tend to bore her. This lady needs stimulation and is sure to find it in abundance with Mr One for a partner. If it's physically possible then this couple are sure to get round to it in the end. It's only a matter of time.

Male One:Female Four

Where personal relationships are concerned this 1:4 combination certainly doesn't look very promising even though it can work moderately well on a business footing. But at close quarters Mr One and Miss Four not only have conflicting personalities, their views and opinions are also completely different and certainly not compatible.

Don't let those sensible shoes and conventional clothes fool you for a moment — Miss Four is a bit of a rebel. She may not dress like a freak, or go around waving a placard bearing a political slogan because that's not her style but she has a peculiar perverse streak in her nature which seems to compel her to see everything from a different angle to everyone else. In arguments she will automatically take the other side. She simply has to reverse the order of everything and has some very odd ideas about social issues and reforms of all kinds. Only when a cause is well and truly lost will she decide to support it and, it goes without saying, that lame dogs are her favourite animals.

There is nothing canine about Mr One and he certainly doesn't limp! He tends to surge at all his targets with great single-mindedness. He looks after number one and doesn't care about other people's struggles and problems unless they happen to threaten his own prospects. Then he'll do something about it.

Already we can see one good reason why Mr One and Miss Four really can't get on. While he's telling everyone to go to blazes she would automatically take their side which would make him appear very foolish indeed when even his own woman won't support him. The ensuing row, when they finally get home, could reach nuclear proportions. And that's another thing, she would almost certainly be for unilateral disarmament and he'd undoubtedly want to keep the bomb. Mr One knows only too well how important it is to keep the balance of power and at that particular moment he would probably decide to push the button if she were anywhere near the target area.

Miss Four likes to do everything to her own strict routine which she's taken years to perfect — Monday washing, Tuesday ironing, Wednesday shopping, etc. It makes her feel secure and she always knows what's going to happen next. So how is she ever going to cope with a spontaneous, impulsive Mr One who likes to do everything on the spur of the moment?

Quite simply — she won't. This 1:4 combination is rather like a time bomb — everyone knows that it's primed and ready to go off but nobody knows quite when the explosion will happen.

Their love life is probably just dull and uneventful. Everything may start off just fine as they'll both be on their best behaviour but as time goes by she'll drift back to the routine curlers, face cream and headaches, not to mention her favourite 'you'll wake the children' ploy and as a result he'll probably lose interest altogether, preferring instead to work late into the night. However, on those rare occasions that their personal needs just happen to coincide their union should be a tender, gentle affair rather than something wild and passionate because, sadly, the earth will never move for a 1:4 combination however hard they try.

Male One:Female Five

When Mr One and Miss Five get together it's rather like putting two champion fighting cocks in the same cage — feathers are bound to fly. Miss Five has the gypsy in her soul. She wants to go everywhere, see everything and sample it too if it looks sufficiently attractive because she's a woman who needs constant stimulation and soon gets bored and fidgety if she can't find something new to do. This same rule applies to the men in her life; once they cease to be amusing they very quickly become yesterday's news.

She probably won't finally decide to settle down in a relationship until well into her late twenties or early thirties by which time she will have seen most of the world and a good few of the men in it too. She'll be very set in her ways by then but will be getting more and more curious about marriage — something she has yet to try. And that's what her life-style really is — one long string of new experiences.

Then along comes unsuspecting Mr One and she can't quite believe her luck. He's such a vital, energetic man. He's charming, rather attractive in a rugged sort of way, so positive in everything he says and does and he certainly doesn't give much away about himself. Emotionally he is very self-controlled which makes him even more of a challenge. 'He's the one for me' she thinks to herself 'but how am I ever going to get him?'

She won't have to — he's spotted her already. But, there again, how could he fail to notice this fascinating creature who has just arrived on the scene? She is not the sort of woman he meets every day — impeccably dressed, hard to analyse, extremely well-informed and very well-travelled. She's perceptive, selective, clever, original and so highly-strung that she must be a real thoroughbred filly. What's more she's adventurous, just like him, and very, very sexy.

The courtship stage of this 1:5 relationship is usually a tempestuous, whirlwind affair and it's a great pity for all concerned that the storm doesn't blow itself out before they decide to take the fatal step and set up home together. While they still have that vital safety valve of a little space between them, which allows sufficient room to manoeuvre, everything is fine. He knows all the best places to go, can always suggest something a little different to do which would be of interest to both of them and he certainly doesn't mind spending his money on meals, entertainment and the odd bunch of flowers or surprise 'un-birthday' presents which she so loves.

Miss Five is also the perfect companion for him. She's unpredictable, which keeps him on his toes and makes sure that his interest doesn't wane, quick-thinking, has an endless store of amusing tales to tell, is always willing to help, although not quite so ready to accept assistance, and likes to live dangerously sometimes, which he finds appealing. He likes a woman with spirit. She also has many hidden talents which he enjoys discovering especially when he finds that they coincide with some of his.

But the trouble starts when they decide to set up home together. She suddenly discovers her wings have been clipped — no more can she follow her flights of fancy and do as she pleases. Now she has to consider someone else and be responsible for her part of the family life. He, on the other hand, can't seem to make her understand that his career is very important to him. He can't spare the time to go out every night to the pub, or to some club or the cinema. He is ambitious, wants to do well for himself and certainly won't get anywhere if he doesn't put his back into his work.

Things could very easily go downhill for this couple unless they take swift and positive action. A compromise must be reached and that really is the burning question here — can they achieve one? If they don't manage to resolve the problem they could find themselves slowly drifting apart with Mr One spending more and more of his time at the office working late and Miss Five doing her own thing with her own circle of friends.

The prospect of this relationship lasting for any length of time certainly doesn't look too hopeful.

Their love life is one thing which might keep them together and if they can forget their differences in each other's arms and lose themselves in their passion things might not look quite so black when they wake up. Mr One is an exciting lover. He's considerate, demonstrative, adventurous and aggressive and as Five is the number of sexuality, the female of the species should be quite a playmate. She would undoubtedly make a very willing accomplice in any of his fantasies.

Male One:Female Six

This combination of a Male One and a Female Six ought to be sub-titled 'Beauty and the Beast'. Although there's nothing really bestial about Mr One he can be domineering and forceful when the mood takes him. Then he likes to throw his weight around and let everyone know exactly who's boss especially at home where he expects to play the role of lord and master. Fortunately he is not nearly as black as he is sometimes painted. He's just the person to have around in an emergency; he rarely panics and calmly and resolutely gets on with what has to be done. He takes his responsibilities very seriously, never tries to avoid doing his duty, is independent, hard-working and overtly ambitious. In fact, he's definitely not such a bad guy after all.

Miss Six certainly lives up to the part she has been chosen to play in this scenario, both in name and in nature. She is kind, loving, artistic, imaginative and altogether a very charming person to have around. She has exquisite taste, can appreciate fine lines and subtle colours like a true connoisseur and is capable of producing some highly original creative work of her own. Besides being talented she is also a very capable woman, a born homemaker and a dedicated wife and mother. Her heart truly lies at home with her family and you can sense this the minute you walk through the front door not only in the calm, peaceful atmosphere she manages to create but also in the beautiful things with which she surrounds herself.

When we put these two individuals together it is really quite surprising to see how well they appear to get along and how much they seem to complement each other. Mr One is addicted to his career and needs regular doses of good, old-fashioned hard work in order to function properly and feel fulfilled and Miss Six certainly won't try to stand in his way. In fact she can very often be a great help to her go-ahead man. She doesn't throw a tantrum or become tight-lipped and uncommunicative when he phones to say he'll be late home again. Naturally she enjoys his company but his absence means that she will have a little bit of extra time to devote to an important project of her own. Never at a loss for something to do, she never complains that time drags when he's working long hours. She enjoys company, has a busy social life of her own and is only too pleased to whip up an impromptu dinner party when he suddenly needs to entertain his boss or some important clients. She is a born hostess.

It cuts both ways for this 1:6 combination. Mr One has a good job with excellent prospects which means that Miss Six isn't forced to go out to work in order to bring in some extra money. So when 'To work, or not to work?' happens to be the question the answer is entirely up to her. She can rely on Mr One because he is responsible and dependable; she won't have to make any major decisions unaided and she knows that she can always turn to him for help and support should she need it. They make a balanced, well-adjusted couple because the give and take in their relationship seems to be in just the right proportions to achieve peace, happiness and a secure future.

But before we leave this combination let's just take a peep around their bedroom door to see if they really are compatible on every level. Mr One is a physical man. He won't ever describe her eyes as deep limpid pools of loveliness or even compare her lips to rose petals because he's not a man who's given to long, poetic speeches; he's more the strong, silent type. But he's very demonstrative and his actions speak for themselves. He's charming, sincere, exciting and, at times, very demanding. He's rather chauvinistic and likes a woman who's meek, servile and obedient for a wife while he secretly lusts after loud, brassy women. Miss Six is affectionate, loyal and faithful. She would certainly set him on a pedestal and probably even 'mother' him but all Sixes are romantics and their love is more chivalrous than sexual in nature. She would certainly fit in with his picture of what a wife should be but she's far too puritanical ever to play the temptress. Fortunately she's not a stupid woman and is quite capable of turning a blind eye to some of her partner's extramarital activities so long as she feels that the basis of love is maintained.

Male One:Female Seven

It should be obvious by now that Ones are rather adventurous individuals who are immediately attracted by anything new and unusual, so it's hardly surprising when Mr One falls under the spell of the mysterious and highly original Miss Seven. She certainly represents a very real challenge and one he is hardly likely to turn down in a hurry.

There is something decidedly different about Miss Seven because she's not like any of the other women he's ever met. She is a clever, intellectual person who can run mental rings around him whenever she chooses. She's definitely not after his money, which makes a refreshing change, and she certainly doesn't give much thought for appearances. Her clothes are old, unfashionable and well-worn but somehow they seem to suit her and tend to add to rather than detract from her appearance.

Mr One has the curiosity of a cat as well as the creative imagination of an artist and this could be one of the main reasons why he finds this woman so fascinating. She's such a loner; she's secretive; in fact, she is a totally unknown quantity and doesn't leave any clues. But she does have a tremendous knowledge and understanding of the occult, philosophy, alternative religions, the mysteries of life, travel, other cultures and life-styles, and could teach him so much about so many things he doesn't understand. He is a man who is always seeking to widen his horizon and gain a much broader view of the world about him and she offers him an opportunity to develop himself even further that he can't possibly afford to miss.

Here again we seem to be looking at a relationship that has something in it from both points of view. While Miss Seven is quite willing to take on Mr One in the role of pupil/soul mate/lover/husband, and also perhaps proffer the odd idea or two which might help him to accellerate his career what can she hope for in return? And the answer is — plenty! Mr One is a powerful, ambitious man with a good steady income which can only improve as he climbs higher and higher up the ladder of success in his chosen profession. Who better to give her the security, financial support, mental stimulation and, of course, love that she needs as well as the time and opportunity to study, research and generally delve further into all the weird and wonderful things that she's so passionately interested in. In fact it looks very much as if she comes out of this deal slightly better off than him — or does she? Perhaps she has more to give.

Mr One, as we already know by now, is a passionate man who even in bed knows what he wants and has charm, flattery, consideration and a few other tricks up his pyjama jacket sleeve to see that his wishes are usually met. But what about the enigmatic Miss Seven? She's certainly not afraid to let her emotions show in private and can be a very sensual woman when roused. She's neither jealous nor possessive so is not likely to cause any ugly scenes on that score, and has such an advanced imagination and powers of intuition that she can probably dream up fantasies faster than they both can act them out. Perhaps there is some truth in the old saying that 'it's the quiet ones you have to watch out for' and Miss Seven seldom makes a sound in public!

Male One:Female Eight

This combination can go only one of two ways — up or down. This is a real battle of giants and we're dealing with two very strong, tough, determined characters in this 1:8 combination.

Mr One is a man who knows his own mind so he probably won't take very kindly to Miss 'Know-It-All' Eight chipping in with her two pennyworth of advice. However, what she's trying to tell him makes very good sense and he knows it. Poor Mr One, he finds her help invaluable but infuriating at the same time. He's a determined and obstinate person who likes to do everything in his own sweet way. It's almost impossible to divert him from a chosen course of action although Miss Eight can somehow manage to do it with convincing reasons and sound arguments. This is a love/hate relationship as far as he is concerned. He undoubtedly loves and admires her but hates the way she always seems to come up with just the right answer.

Miss Eight, on the other hand, can be just as tenacious, aggressive and stubborn and she, too, knows exactly what she wants from life and how to get it. She needs to succeed more than anything else and, what's more, she has to be seen to do so. When a One and an Eight get together in any relationship they always have to try to outdo each other. And unless they can both control their forceful natures the whole situation can turn from one of healthy rivalry to a fight to the death, with no holds barred.

Unfortunately, if these two should ever seriously fall out they are both far too proud and headstrong ever to consider saying 'sorry' or even 'can we try again?' The partnership would be liquidated immediately and the assets divided out with absolutely no show of emotion from him and a brusque, business-like attitude from her. Hopefully matters won't be allowed to deteriorate to such a stage but, sadly, divorce and separation are fairly common endings for a 1:8 relationship.

In their bedroom, or anywhere else for that matter provided it's private and no one else is going to come barging in, Mr One is an exciting lover. He's charming, demonstrative, passionate and experimental although, at times, he can be a little selfish, expecting to receive more than he can be bothered to give especially when he's been working extra hard. But in this particular 1:8 union he is not the problem. Eight is a number of extremes and when Miss Eight is in the mood she can make love all night but when she's not Mr One might just as well turn over and go to sleep because nothing will rouse her. Somehow she can never quite reach the point where her sexual desire becomes balanced. And there is another thing which Mr One will pretty soon discover about this lady; she suffers from an incurable disease known as rampant jealousy for which there is no known cure. So even if they both manage to control their natural antagonism in public her private affliction which causes her to see everything in shades of green could well sound the final death knell for this dynamic twosome.

Male One:Female Nine

There can be no doubt at all that this relationship will flourish despite the fact that Mr One has a very forceful, dominant personality because Miss Nine is one of that rare breed of women who can disagree without anger and reach a working compromise with a certain degree of humour. In other words, she can usually get what she wants without causing too much trouble.

She is the ideal companion for Mr One; she's not simply some decorative piece of furniture standing around the place waiting to do his bidding although she will try to make him as happy as possible and fall in with his wishes in most things — she is also a woman with intelligence, a fine brain and opinions of her own. This means that she can not only discuss matters with him on equal terms, but she can also understand some of the problems he encounters at work and can offer useful suggestions or constructive criticism. But woe betide him should he ever find fault with any of her ideas, then it's quite a different story. She's not actually conceited but she does have a very high opinion of herself and will brook no interference however well-meant. So unless he has praise or encouragement to offer it would be better if he held his tongue and said nothing at all. Let her make her own mistakes; that's the way she prefers things.

Mr One has two great loves in his life, his woman and his work, and very often his work appears to be the more important of the two. Some women could find this tiresome but not Miss Nine; she will probably have an interesting career of her own to follow and can always find something to occupy herself with when she does have some time on her hands. She's amusing, good company, easy to get along with, a stimulating conversationalist and will undoubtedly have a great many friends and acquaintances outside this relationship who share her interests. All Nines, irrespective of sex, have wide sympathies and an intense urge to serve in some worthwhile cause.

This arrangement suits Mr One just fine. He likes to be left alone to get on with things in peace without someone constantly nagging or reminding him of all the things around the house that still need to be done. He's ambitious, single-minded, self-reliant and certainly doesn't need any encouragement to get on with his work. He's obstinate, determined and very set in his ways so he gets on well with Miss Nine because she seems to like him just the way he is. She is loyal, unselfish, successful in her own right, and doesn't keep running to him for support when things go wrong for her. She is a courageous, enterprising woman who can stand on her own two feet and Mr One has great admiration for anyone who can do that and, naturally, he includes himself in this category.

This relationship works even better, if that's possible, in the privacy of their own home than its does in daily life. Mr One could never be described as a 'sleepy' sleeping-partner, he's a very red-blooded, sensual man who always leaves his partner thinking that he has kept something of himself in reserve to be discovered and enjoyed at some later date.

Miss Nine may be very worried over world problems and shortages during the day but at night she's only concerned about two very special people and no one goes without in this private world she shares with Mr One; she will see to that. She's a passionate woman who's not afraid to show her feelings or make her demands known and she is more than a match for Mr One any day although he would never admit it.

Male Two:Female One

'Just give me a couple of minutes to unwind first' he'll plead as she tosses him an apron and presses a duster into his hands the minute he comes in through the door. And she should show more consideration for this man because he has so much to offer especially when he's the other half of a career-minded Miss One. She'll get far more from this relationship with kid glove tactics than she ever will if she nags and continually orders him around. 'Please' and 'thank you' would be useful words to add to her vocabulary and they should be used frequently.

Mr Two is sensitive and lacks confidence in himself. He is quiet, indecisive and unambitious but he's a willing helper, a good listener and, above all, he wants the woman who shares his life to be happy. He derives much of his pleasure second-hand through watching his loved ones get on and do well for themselves. He'd be proud to have a partner like Miss One and would do anything he could to help her succeed. He would be supportive, understanding and certainly wouldn't dream of trying to stop her following her career. His woman's place is only in the home if that is where she prefers to be. But if she wants to work then it's fine by him provided he's never given cause to doubt her love or fidelity for even a second. Sadly, Mr Two is the original green-eyed monster; he's the personification of jealousy and its runs right through him from the top of his head to the very tips of his toes. Most of his torment is unnecessary and self-inflicted. It stems largely from his vivid imagination and general feelings of insecurity — perhaps if he had a better opinion of himself this would never happen.

Any woman could be forgiven for finding him trying at times and Miss One, who's not known for being the most patient person in the world, could find her temper wearing rather thin when he pouts and sulks after yet another outburst of accusations. Even if she were like Caesar's wife

— above suspicion — he would still manage to find something to suspect. Unless he can somehow manage to control this negative emotion or she is prepared to turn a deaf ear it could eventually destroy this relationship by a steady process of erosion.

However, Miss One has some room for improvement if she doesn't want to emasculate Mr Two totally and turn him into a hen-pecked husband; even if she wears the metaphorical trousers at home, she should be less demeaning in public. She needs to adopt a softer, more feminine approach and should keep a tight rein on that aggressive, 'me first' attitude of hers which could well get her somewhere at work but will only serve to harm her relationship with a shy, romantic Mr Two.

The intimate side of this partnership could be a source of joy and pleasure to them both. Mr Two is tender, romantic, considerate, imaginative — in fact, he'll do anything to please, while Miss One is lively, demonstrative, adventurous and certainly not afraid to take the initiative.

Provided she doesn't become over aggressive and make Mr Two feel he has taken on rather more than he can cope with, this relationship can work well for both partners on all levels.

Male Two:Female Two

Two plus two doesn't only equal four, it is also a numerological formula for perfect happiness. Mr Two and Miss Two were meant for each other because they are almost identical in every way. They could be two peas from the same pod and all they want to do is please each other.

Mr Two is an even-tempered man who lacks the drive and confidence to go far in the world of business and commerce. He probably has a very ordinary 'nine to five' job which entails few responsibilities and offers very little in the way of prospects, but it is steady, secure and suits him down to the ground. No worries, few problems and no extra work to take home and finish in the evenings. There's nothing dynamic, forceful or even particularly positive about him but in her eyes he's a god in mortal form and her whole world revolves around him.

Once these two have managed to conquer their shyness and get to know one another they'll find they get on like a house on fire. Who else could understand the way they both feel better than another of their own number? They won't have to make excuses for feeling self-conscious at times, neither will they have to give an explanation for their changeable moods because they both know how agonizingly difficult life can be for people born under this number.

When they finally decide to take the plunge and get married, she will probably give up her routine job (Miss Two's never have careers). She can then devote herself and all her time to looking after her Mr Two. And she makes an excellent wife because she's a good organizer (but always on a very limited scale), careful with money and what's more she's one of that dying breed of women who thoroughly enjoy being 'just a housewife' and nothing more. She may secretly yearn for a microwave oven or a split-level cooker but never for a high-powered job, a pay cheque of her own or the independence that some of her friends seem to have.

Mr and Miss Two have something very special going for them which most couples never experience no matter how long they've been together. Many Twos possess some form of ESP which can take the form of clairvoyance, clairaudience, psychometry and so on, but when they get together they seem to develop a unique form of telepathy and can communicate mentally with each other even over great distances and, on extreme occasions, from opposite sides of the world. But this is rarely put to the test because Twos do tend to stay very close to each other once a relationship has grown between them.

However there's a darker side to a Two's nature which needs to be kept under very close control especially in this 2:2 relationship where it comes in a double helping. They can both be suspicious, cruel and deceitful at times, not to mention fractious, jealous and very depressed.

In private (and it will have to be so very private for these two shy, sensitive souls to feel relaxed) the expression of their love will be like something out of a fairy tale with the handsome prince finally carrying his beautiful princess off to his castle high on a hill on his fiery white steed. Twos are incurable romantics, tender, compassionate and considerate. They need to be constantly reassured of each other's love and provided they are they can both live happily ever after like royal lovers in a story book.

Male Two:Female Three

'What ever does she see in him?' is quite a natural question and one people frequently ask when Mr Two and Miss Three decide to team up. She is talented, versatile and lively while he is quiet and painfully self-conscious.

She does, in fact, find many things which initially attract her to Mr Two but this is not going to be an easy relationship to maintain for either of them. Only a super-human effort will keep them together for long. Because, as time goes by and she gets to know him better, she is bound to discover many things about him which are definitely not to her liking. And from where she stands the pros could eventually become heavily outweighed by the cons. At this point she will probably decide to call it a day — Miss Three is not one to hang around once she has become disenchanted with a partner.

She's always been rather a theatrical person at heart so she should find the first half of this production extremely enjoyable. But when the curtain comes down for the interval and the two star performers retire to their dressing rooms to assess their performances the second act could suddenly turn from a piece of light-hearted entertainment into a heavy drama. He can be such a kind, thoughtful man, always willing to help, always the first to make up an argument and always ready to listen to her troubles so why does he have to spoil everything with his peculiar, changeable moods, his black depressions and his terrible jealousy? He is forever checking up on her in such sly, underhand ways and his cruel accusations and emotional outbursts are more than any faithful woman would be prepared to suffer. And so what started out as a happy, caring relationship gradually turns into a terrible mistake which she wants to escape from as soon as possible.

However, there are always two sides to every story so let's look at this 2:3 relationship from his point of view. At first he can hardly believe his ears when this proud, independent woman says she would be delighted to dine with him tomorrow evening. It has taken him days to pluck up sufficient courage to ask her out and then he starts worrying whether the restaurant he has chosen will be good enough and how he should impress her.

Fortunately, as their relationship develops, he does manage to overcome his initial awkwardness and begins to feel more relaxed in her company. He finds her shrewd, imaginative, witty, creative and utterly charming but then he begins to notice that other men think the same.

This is when the rot sets in. He has always doubted his own worth and begins to wonder what she gets up to when he isn't around, who she sees at work, did she really visit a girlfriend last Thursday? — and so on. He needs her so much and can't bear the thought of anyone or anything else coming between them. He becomes more and more intolerant, possessive, critical and withdrawn while she becomes angry and defensive one minute and then treats the whole thing as some enormous joke the next.

Once matters have reached this stage something has to give and it's usually her. She's like her symbol, the otter, in this respect. She'll amuse, charm, show off, captivate and enthral her audience in her natural surroundings but try to confine her movements or restrict her freedom in any way and she'll be off in the twinkling of an eye.

When things are going well between them, the intimate side of this relationship is usually a source of comfort to both parties. He's tender, romantic and gentle and she's warm, considerate and sufficiently adaptable to fit in with his constantly changing moods. When he is feeling low she has a way of making him laugh at his troubles and when he's on a high she will enjoy it with him. But when the differences between them start to get out of hand he will be far too busy cultivating a really good sulk to even notice that she is already fast asleep.

It really is a shame that a combination which initially offers such promise and hope for the future usually ends up in this way with one partner feeling bitterly hurt and disappointed and the other deciding to put the whole disastrous episode down to experience.

Male Two:Female Four

A personal relationship between Mr Two and Miss Four always runs smoothly because it's so well-balanced. Disagreements seldom arise but when they do they're quickly settled and soon forgotten. Harmony is undoubtedly a keyword for this combination.

Mr Two is not a forceful, dynamic man who takes life by storm or goes to any lengths to ensure that he succeeds, in fact he's quite the opposite. He's quiet, tactful and conciliatory, finding anger and discord very distressing. He's rather shy and self-conscious and will always try to wriggle out of making a decision when he possibly can. But when he finally has to make up his mind he will probably only change it again a few minutes later.

Miss Four, on the other hand, is a born organizer. She will be only too pleased to get him into some sort of routine and will soon sort out all his problems in her own methodical way. She is such a down-to-earth woman and views obstacles in her path as mere irritations which simply have to be overcome. She's calm, efficient, industrious, practical and handles money wisely and with a certain amount of respect. She is well aware that it doesn't grow on trees and because Mr Two hasn't got a job which commands a vast salary she knows that one of them has to be realistic about their finances and see that something is put away for a rainy day. You can count on her to do that — she needs to feel secure and a healthy bank balance always means a happy, more relaxed Miss Four.

Mr Two is a sensitive man, he'll compromise rather than argue a point. Easily swayed by people and circumstances, he'll usually bend with the prevailing wind rather than make a stand on his own. In any case he never really feels so strongly about a matter that he's prepared to fight for it and because of this he will usually always be a subordinate, never a leader. However, he does have a gentle nature, a superb imagination and a romantic outlook on life which could greatly influence Miss Four and open up a whole new dimension to her — the mental rather than her usual physical plane of experience. She is solid and steady, but he is a man who could lift her into new realms of thought and together they could explore his world of dreams where only beauty and peace exist. Initially she could find this difficult because she's not a fanciful woman but given sufficient time and encouragement she'll soon discover a side to her personality which has been laying dormant for far too long. All it needed was the right key — in the shape of Mr Two — to enable her to unlock her finer feelings.

Unfortunately, Mr Two has some feelings of his own which would be better locked away. He's a moody person and quickly gets despondent and depressed over trivialities. He tends to imagine the most awful things which are never really likely to happen and is far too easily wounded by an ill-chosen remark or even a stern glare when he is liable to withdraw into a reproachful silence. And to make matters worse, he's also jealous and possessive. But strangely enough his negative behaviour seems to cut no ice with Miss Four. Once she had listened to his grievances she soon finds him something to do which will take his mind off the subject — and this approach seems to work. While he's busy chopping firewood or mowing the lawn he becomes more concerned with the task in hand than about her imaginary lover or the way his boss dressed him down. She has most definitely got the measure of him!

In the privacy of their own home, harmony is still a keyword. Mr Two is an incorrigible romantic, a knight in shining armour who wants to serve his fair lady and make her ecstatically happy. He is caring, tender, compassionate, chivalrous and uses fine words and gentle kisses to demonstrate his feelings towards her. And all can be sweetness and light between them because she is a woman who needs to feel loved, is capable of great depths of feeling and also of expressing herself physically but somehow without the aggression which would put him off. However, when he's just started reciting the eighth verse of yet another epic poem he's written for her she must never, ever be tempted to remark that the room could do with a coat of paint or ask if he's put out the dustbin. Practical and organized she may well be but that would be a cardinal error on her part. It would shatter everything in an instant and she may not get him to utter another word for days, or even weeks, after such a blow to his psyche.

Male Two:Female Five

Mr Two had better enjoy this relationship while it lasts because the prospects for a long-term association look far from good — unless, of course, he's prepared to alter his image completely and undergo a personality change at the same time.

Miss Five is an adventurous woman. She's cool, capable and extremely efficient at taking care of herself. She's restless, unpredictable and almost impossible to pin down even for five minutes at a time. She wants freedom of mind, body and spirit and needs to travel widely in order to gain as much first-hand experience of life as possible. So what chance does poor Mr Two stand when he seems to be competing against the whole world for her attention? Sadly, he'll never be able to change in time for this impatient lady. She'll be up and away long before he's even learned to speak a little louder or with greater authority.

She must have seen something in him which initially attracted her. Unfortunately, in a 2:5 relationship, it's usually a case of mistaken identity. She mistook his silence for strength, his even temper for great self-control and found his shyness refreshing rather than infuriating as it later becomes when she gets to know him better. In fact, when she suddenly realizes that initially she had summed him up all wrong, she won't wait around to see if anything can be salvaged from the wreckage of this relationship, she'll simply pack her bags and continue on her merry way without as much as a backward glance.

And even if everything else was satisfactory between these two, which it's not, their empty bedroom is the final testament to the unsuitability of this union. Mr Two, as we already know, is a romantic. Love for him tends to be a state of mind rather than something which he cares to demonstrate physically. He goes in for fine words, long meaningful glances and discreet kisses. He loves from a distance rather than at close quarters and Miss Five certainly won't settle for that. Hers is the number sexuality and she wants action not words; they won't keep her warm at night unless she decides to set fire to his poetry books. She's a sensual, liberated woman who needs a red-blooded man of action, not a timid, moody mouse, to satisfy her demands. In short, this combination just doesn't work!

Male Two:Female Six

These two peaceloving individuals may not set the business world aflame because they both lack drive and aggression but they instinctively know how to keep their own homefire burning and each other blissfully happy. The sensitive Red Admiral butterfly (Mr Two) and his white dove of peace (Miss Six) make a handsome, well-matched pair. And they seem positively to flourish in the quiet, restful atmosphere which they create around them.

Two is a neutral number which can be good or bad depending on the prevailing circumstances. It means that Mr Two is rather inclined to be influenced by the people he mixes with and also by his surroundings. In this particular relationship Miss Six has a very beneficial effect. She seems to bring out the best in him and together they can discover a side to his nature which has hitherto never been fully developed.

Miss Six is a talented woman; she is interested in painting, music, sculpture, writing and so many other things besides. She has an eye for colour, loves beautiful things, has many 'arty' intelligent friends and simply adores her home, where she likes to spend the majority of her time. She's imaginative, well-balanced, self-controlled, sympathetic and at her best when involved in some kind of creative activity.

Deep down Mr Two is also an imaginative, creative person but he has such a massive inferiority complex that he thinks people will laugh if he takes up the cello or that they'll criticise his primitive attempts at landscape painting. He's got an eggshell ego and an ill-chosen remark could put him off for ever. In fact, he's so afraid of other people's negative reactions and comments that he usually never gets started, having already pre-judged the outcome. But with Miss Six at his side all this silly self-doubt will have to be put to one side because she can see that he has something worth developing. She will soon coax, bully and cajole him into using his talents; she's a persuasive lady who can be very determined at times.

She also loves to entertain family and friends; she wants to make everyone about her happy and to bring some pleasure into their lives. She prefers to give small, informal suppers rather than stiff, starchy dinner parties and once Mr Two gets over his initial shyness he'll soon find himself enjoying these occasions enormously because that competitive element of rivalry which he dislikes so much at work simply doesn't arise at one of her little parties. So, perhaps rather slowly at first, he begins to come out of his shell. He finds her friends interesting and entertaining and what's more they seem to find him so, and he becomes even more relaxed in their company. This does wonders for his undernourished ego and gradually the metamorphosis takes places; the dull, boring, brown crysallis opens up and the highly coloured, extremely attractive adult butterfly emerges.

Miss Six can certainly work wonders for her man and in return she gains a loyal, loving partner who will go to any lengths to make her happy. Only his jealousy remains dormant in this relationship, because she is far too open and loyal to doubt; everything else about him is awakened, taken out, dusted down and well-aired. He becomes a different, better person under her influence and even his changeable moods seem to balance out in the fullness of time.

The expression of their love is bound to be a beautiful experience for both of them. He is so tender and romantic, says such wonderful things and has a way of looking at her which she finds irresistible. He's a caring, gentle man. She too leans to the romantic and ideal in all matters of the heart and sees love as something to be treasured and spoken about rather than of a purely physical nature. She's kind, affectionate, considerate although at times rather inclined to 'mother' her man but Mr Two probably enjoys this anyway so, in this particular relationship, it won't do any great harm.

There's little doubt that Mr Two and Miss Six have a great deal going for them.

Male Two:Female Seven

There's something very spiritual about the entire set-up when Mr Two and Miss Seven decide to join forces. In fact, without the occasional burst of friction that he is bound to inject from time to time, this relationship could be too peaceful and harmonious for its own good.

Miss Seven is sweet-natured, pleasant and hates arguments. She's intelligent, reserved, highly imaginative and creative. So far, so good — Mr Two is completely in tune with this side of her nature but there lies the rub — she can also be very secretive and often likes to go off on her own which is something he simply can't cope with. Why won't she tell him what she's up to, where she has been and what she writes in that notebook of hers? It's all perfectly innocent but he probably wouldn't believe her even if she told him. He pictures imaginary lovers every time the telephone rings for her and always prefers to think the worst of even the most harmless situation.

When he's not accusing her of gadding about with other men or letting the house go to rack and ruin, relations between them can be very good. He, like her, is creative, sensitive and imaginative and she's always full of weird and wonderful theories to discuss, philosophical views to air or strange religious beliefs to investigate. If he could only get it into his head that she's only interested in him and that she has neither the time nor the inclination to dally with other men, then all will be well. But if provoked beyond endurance she is quite capable of ending their relationship with considerable coldness.

He is tender, kind, considerate and noble while she's fascinating, mysterious, challenging and elusive at one and the same time. She is also a passionate woman and rather inclined to take the lead which he could find slightly unnerving at first but he soon gets used to being interrupted in the middle of one of his long, flowery speeches by his impatient lady.

Provided Mr Two keeps his jealousy very tightly in check and Miss Seven doesn't spend too much time in that world of her own this relationship can be a rewarding experience for both parties.

Male Two:Female Eight

In a 2:8 relationship Miss Eight does all the pushing and Mr Two resists every inch of the way. Even on those rare occasions when he does give in and do as he's told he won't have heard the last of it because she'll soon have her sights on something else for him to achieve.

He saw so much in her at first, which is still there, but perhaps his glasses needed changing because there are other things about her which he certainly didn't notice until it was too late. She is strong, practical and wise, just the sort of woman he could rely on to back him up and bolster his ego. She's responsible, hard-working, organized and seems to be able to overcome anything that gets in her way. Unfortunately he is often the obstacle in her path. She wants everything she's involved in to turn out to perfection, including her marriage. It's also a good thing she has a career of her own and perhaps earns more than he does otherwise they would never manage to keep her in the style to which she quickly becomes accustomed. Mr Two is self-conscious and feels inferior at the best of times and her attitude towards his earning capacity certainly doesn't help to boost his morale one iota.

She frequently wonders what she ever saw in him because he's so touchy when she tries to advise him, flies into a rage at the slightest criticism, changes his mind every five minutes and broods for far too long over every silly little mistake he makes. She forgets what a good listener he used to be when she had something interesting to say, how kind and considerate he was when she had that spell in hospital or indeed, how refreshingly different he seemed from all those pushy, aggressive men she crosses swords with every day in her work.

If only he would lay down the law a bit more often and she would stop and consider his feelings occasionally their relationship could be restored to the way it was. However, things usually go the opposite way.

To make matters worse they're both insanely jealous but she at least tries to conceal the fact which is more than he does. It's a wonder they stay together but perhaps the saying 'old habits die hard' is true in their case, because they are both inclined to be set in their ways. They've probably grown so used to the situation that eventually they accept it as the normal way of life.

Their private life too will probably be far from 'normal' although this doesn't mean that either of them are sexual deviants or fetishists. Miss Eight might worship the great god Mammon but she does manage to leave her money under the mattress and never takes it into bed with her, although she may sneak off occasionally to count it when he's asleep. Eight is a number of extremes so she will either be very much in the mood for lovemaking or she won't want to know. And when she's feeling totally disinterested nothing will ever persuade her to change her mind.

Mr Two sees love as an ideal to be worshipped and cherished and when she decides to sleep in another room because his snoring keeps her awake so much the better. Then he can worship her from afar and cherish his memories on his own. Not a very inspiring picture generally but on those rare occasions when their emotions do happen to coincide and they're both in the proper frame of mind for a physical demonstration of their feelings, then the floor has been known to tremble slightly.

Male Two:Female Nine

Faith, hope and charity are all present in varying degrees in this particular combination. Mr Two has great faith in Miss Nine and sincerely hopes that their relationship will be a source of joy to them both. Nine is certainly the most charitable of all the Love Numbers and those ruled by it have a great love for mankind. They are kind and affectionate, liberal in giving, lenient in judgement and very understanding. This partnership seems to be off to a very good start.

Even in these times of so-called equality Miss Nine still finds herself wishing she had been born a man. She fondly imagines that if this had been the case she could have done so much more to improve the living standards and conditions of ordinary men and women all over the globe. She is a woman of vision. She has big ideas and an even bigger heart to promote them. Then along comes Mr Two and she suddenly feels very glad that she is a woman after all.

He seems too quiet and shy at first but when she gets to know him better she soon discovers all manner of fascinating things about him. He may not be decisive and dynamic; admittedly he's moody and difficulty to handle at times but deep down he really cares and that's what she likes most of all.

In turn he thinks the world of her because she seems to embody all the qualities he has looked for in a woman. She is stimulating, inspiring and extremely attractive and while she may not be a classical beauty she has great charm and an air of dignity about her which many women try to ape but only a few actually achieve. She is honest, trusting, resourceful and always stands by what she says. If she makes a promise she will keep it. When she vows to be his faithful wife it never crosses his jealous mind to doubt her for a moment.

Miss Nine has found herself a man who actually understands what she is trying to do and he has found himself a very special woman who seems able to live with his changeable moods, his hesitancy and his sensitivity without complaint.

Miss Nine is easy to get along with in any situation, but when the lights are low and there's no one else around except Mr Two, she becomes even more charming and affectionate than usual. She is passionate, warm, trusting and loyal with a deep craving for love and a physical show of affection to go with it. Mr Two is a romantic at heart; he's tender, caring, considerate and, above all, willing to please. Neither party should have reason to complain too bitterly or often about this liaison although if anyone does it will probably be Miss Nine because, at times, he may not be demonstrative enough for her liking. She is quite prepared to go along with all his beautiful words and meaningful glances provided that action follows later but when their lovemaking begins to turn into one long poetry reading after another you can be sure she'll have a few well-chosen words of her own to say about the matter.

Male Three:Female One

Very often in life it's the people who are prepared to take the greatest risks who stand to reap the greatest rewards and that happens with this particular combination — they will find their time together stimulating, exciting, challenging and definitely fast-moving.

Miss One is certainly not one of those mousey little women who have nothing to say for themselves. She is attractive, charming, capable and career-minded. She is likely to have a highly-paid, responsible job and her prospects are excellent. She's positive, original, intelligent, tenacious and extremely self-controlled. She knows her own mind and seldom needs to seek advice or encouragement from others.

Mr Three is a talented man with a shrewd, clever mind which can concentrate on several different things at the same time. He is observant, lively, imaginative, versatile and very witty. He's also very ambitious, which Miss One likes in a man, exceptionally independent, which she understands, and incredibly lucky, which she can't quite believe. He is far too changeable and adaptable for her ever to find him dull; he's a dozen different people all rolled into one and so she never quite knows from one day to the next what he is going to be like or what he'll do next to keep her guessing.

However, as we already know, we all have negative as well as positive sides to our characters. These two are certainly no exceptions to this rule. Miss One can be very bossy and stubborn at times; she likes to have her own way and hates to be restricted or told what to do by someone else.

Mr Three can also be an old show-off at times, and she won't find that easy to live with unless, of course, it's her he happens to be showing off to his friends. Then she'll just smile sweetly and pretend she hasn't noticed. But what will really make her mad is his inability to take anything seriously because there are some things in life (her career and her ideas to name but two) about which she never jokes.

Generally this couple should get along very well together most of the time because they are both lively, intelligent people who can only fully share their thoughts and feelings with someone of their own mental capacity. Good looks alone won't do for either of them for very long; they both need a partner who has brains as well and in this 3:1 combination the balance is tipped very much in their favour. Miss One finds her partner a challenge because he can do so many things well and she can't bear to be outshone by anyone while he adores her wild, adventurous nature. He admires a woman who will stand on her own two feet and who isn't afraid to take opportunities when they arise.

In private this pair are even more daring and imaginative than ever. He's an exciting, resourceful man who never allows his lovemaking to become routine or predictable. He is full of surprises, and love, and fun. Just like his symbol the otter he is bold, amusing, versatile and utterly charming. And Miss One certainly isn't slow at coming forward; there's nothing shy or modest about her. She's all woman and she deserves only the very best . . . and what's more, she'll get it even if its does mean taking the initiative occasionally. She needs a very special man indeed to keep her happy and Mr Three will do very nicely.

Male Three:Female Two

Mr Three and Miss Two are rather like the first and second violins in an orchestra. They both have their separate parts to play in this relationship but when combined the result is perfect harmony. As long as Miss Two is prepared to play second fiddle while Mr Three controls the brilliant and charming tune, then all will be well but there is no reason to believe that she'll ever want to do anything else because most Twos prefer to take a secondary role in life as they perhaps lack the self-confidence and drive required to take the lead.

Mr Three, on the other hand, is versatile and ambitious, highly talented and can do many things well. He's lively, adaptable, shrewd, observant, original and likely to be very successful in life because he has that element of luck as well as good judgement in his favour. Miss Two is rather a timid person, so Mr Three is good for her in many ways. He is strong and protective, which means that she can turn to him for support whenever she feels the need to lean on someone. He is an extrovert so nobody will really notice how quiet she is when he's around and because he's such an intelligent, shrewd man he can give her just the right sort of encouragement to help her to make better use of her undeniably creative talents. And, what's more, he's so easy-going that he's unlikely to take her changeable moods too seriously. He is probably the one person who can jolly her along and take her mind off all her imaginary problems without making a drama of the whole issue. How can she possibly get a good depression going when he keeps making her giggle?

The give and take cuts both ways in this personal relationship because she can also do a lot for him. She is a good listener and he does love to talk about anything, everything and himself in particular. She is sweet-natured, loyal, tactful and always willing to help him in any way she can. She has good judgement even though she is rather indecisive some of the time. And she is always the first to try to end an argument and certainly knows how to reach a working compromise. Miss Two enjoys having company and Mr Three has many friends he likes to entertain. This is when she really does him proud. She's a good hostess, an imaginative cook and the perfect partner for an independent man because she never tries to push anything on him which he doesn't want. What's more, she'd never dream of questioning either his authority or his motives.

The intimate side of this 3:2 relationship should also be relatively trouble-free for both parties. Mr Three isn't particularly jealous or possessive. In love he can be loyal, warm and tender without getting too passionate or over-demonstrative because this would rather unsettle the sensitive, modest Miss Two. He is also shrewd and observant which means that he can sense what mood she's in without having to be told. The lady in this scenario is a caring, devoted person although she is rather inclined to feel insecure every so often and needs constant reassurance of her partner's undying love. A considerate, incurable romantic, she likes to be cuddled, fussed and told lots of nice things about herself. While they may not be the most adventurous pair of lovers they are certainly one of the happiest because neither of them expects too much or places too great an importance on the physical side of their union. They just want to be together and anything else they derive from their partnership comes as an added bonus.

Male Three:Female Three

Anything at all which involves two Threes will be a risk, whether it's a financial venture or something of a more personal nature, simply because they're reckless, headstrong individuals who trust far too much to luck and not enough to judgement. This is a combination of gamblers and the odds on this couple remaining together for any length of time are not favourable. Unless both parties learn to become more responsible and reflective their relationship will not stand much of a chance.

Mr Three is a talented man who achieves many things, but because he's so lively and changeable he rarely settles at anything for long. He is always afraid of missing out on something else which could be even more fun and so he becomes a Jack of all trades and master of none. He has a fine brain, some brilliant ideas, expresses himself boldly and vividly but just can't settle down. He always seems to be one jump ahead of everyone, including himself. Probably the most infuriating thing of all is that fact that he won't take anything seriously. If people were like playing cards then he would be the joker in the pack — you never know when he's going to turn up or what effect he will have on the hand that has been dealt.

Miss Three is an independent woman who likes to come and go as she pleases. She's easy-going, friendly and utterly charming. She has a quick brain, the luck of the devil and nine lives just like the proverbial cat. She is versatile, clever, imaginative and artistically gifted but, unfortunately, just like her male counterpart, she can never settle down to anything for long before she becomes bored, restless and starts looking around for something new to take her fancy.

Threes of both sexes are proud, refined individuals who often care a great deal about what others think of them. They tend to chafe under the least restraint, dislike being under an obligation to others and are inclined to be dictatorial. They are obstinate and also very outspoken which can sometimes give offence. Tact and discretion are not their strong points. They need a great deal of personal freedom and for this reason they often find that joint ventures are too restrictive. So when we have a combination like this it's not really surprising that it seldom works because they are both tarred with the same brush.

Even the intimate side of this relationship soon becomes stale as they are really too much alike to hold each other's interest for very long. Neither is jealous, neither is possessive, in fact, neither really seems to care very much one way or another in the end. They can both be warm, exciting and impulsive when the mood takes them but, like their symbol the otter, when the situation ceases to be amusing they are gone in a flash without so much as a backwards glance.

Male Three:Female Four

Allowances will have to be made and a working compromise sought if this combination of numbers is to get anywhere at all. The main problem here is the fact that Mr Three and Miss Four have very little in common, other than a purely physical attraction, and any relationship needs rather more to keep it on the right road. However, if they were to cultivate a few shared interests and somehow manage to overcome the more obvious personality differences which exist between them, then there is no real reason why a stable personal relationship shouldn't develop. At the end of the day the final outcome will be determined by the amount of effort that both parties are prepared to make and, indeed, by how much they really care about each other.

Mr Three is brilliant, imaginative and versatile but he is also rather inclined to take risks or act on the spur of the moment, so the cautious Miss Four will need to make allowances. He is lively, charming, observant and shrewd, none of which should cause her any problems, but he does have a very quick mind and she could find his way of being one jump ahead slightly disconcerting. He is easy-going, friendly, highly talented especially in the arts and full of original ideas which are all to the good until we reach another 'but' — he is also obstinate, singularly proud, occasionally dictatorial and tends to chafe under the least restraint. Again Miss Four will need to handle him with kid gloves if she wants to get her own way. Mr Three is extremely clever with words and could run rings around her in a battle of wits so she should avoid verbal sparring whenever possible. He will usually emerge as the victor.

Miss Four is solid, practical, down-to-earth and virtually unflappable. In fact she takes life rather seriously which is something Mr Three rarely does. Here is one area where they are bound to clash from time to time. She is efficient, well-organized, hard-working and good with money. No problems here until we find that she simply can't bear waste and he is one of the world's worst for leaving food half-eaten or throwing away a perfectly serviceable pair of trousers. But she does possess a fine brain, her conversation is interesting, she has a fund of amusing stories to tell and an infectious laugh to go with them. Once he has taken the trouble to look behind that rather dull, humourless, respectable face she presents to the world he will very soon discover what fun she can be when she's 'off-duty' and relaxed.

When we come to the physical, rather personal side of this combination, which is probably what prompted them to get together in the first place, we find that things work well between them. No major changes or adjustments should be necessary as they seem to have the formula right. Once Miss Four has experienced the love of this man her private life should be more exciting, varied and interesting than ever before. He is demonstrative, loyal, warm, impulsive and a very caring man to have as a lover. Miss Four is also a considerate woman, sentimental, faithful and capable of great depths of feeling. She needs to feel loved and secure at all times and Mr Three can offer her these things. Neither of them are particularly jealous or possessive by nature and problems rarely occur in the private part of this relationship.

Male Three:Female Five

There's never a dull moment when Mr Three and Miss Five get together — any spectators watching from the sidelines certainly won't need to rely on television soap operas for their entertainment. This couple should provide them with more than enough action while their relationship lasts. Both are very lively, restless, impatient, extrovert individuals and their partnership could suffer if they try to burn the candle at both ends. After that first mad fling one of them will need to apply the brakes from time to time if they hope to remain together for very long.

Mr Three is just what the doctor ordered for Miss Five so long as she remembers to stick to the prescribed dose and doesn't overstep the mark. He is a charming, witty man who expresses himself boldly and vividly. He has a fine brain, plenty of original ideas and is talented in many directions. He's also a happy, gifted character who never lets things get him down because he rarely takes anything that seriously. Mr Three is adaptable, easy-going, impulsive and extremely lucky. He knows how to enjoy himself and is tremendous fun to be with — in fact, he's the very man for Miss Five.

But in this relationship Miss Five tends to act as a catalyst. She's the one who sets everything in motion and for this reason she is also the one who can make or break the situation. She is a fidgety, adventurous woman who loves taking risks and and will try anything that appeals to her simply because it's different. She does so hate to feel in a rut! She will kick against anything which becomes restrictive or routine; she must always feel free to come and go as she pleases. The worst thing Mr Three could ever do is try to tie this woman down; once he becomes too possessive or attempts to clip her wings and quieten her in any way she will be off in an instant. She is very quick in thought and decision and extremely impulsive in her actions. Breathing space is what she needs and that's what he will have to give her unless he wants to lose her for good. But if he can fulfil this important condition then all should be well between them.

Miss Five craves excitement and Mr Three is certainly not averse to trying something a little eccentric or unusual in his spare time. On one level these two have never really grown up because neither can resist the other's 'challenges' and their relationship often becomes an adult variation of the childhood game of dares. When he says 'Oh no, you wouldn't — would you?' he knows very well what her answer will be and she only has to suggest that maybe he's getting a bit middle-aged and boring to having him eating out of her hand and raring to go. This is why restraint is so necessary in this 3:5 combination because without it they could burn each other out in a matter of months.

The daring, 'anything goes' attitude which exists in this relationship certainly continues in private where, if anything, it becomes intensified. Mr Three is a healthy, red-blooded man and behind locked doors Miss Five is no lady. She's a sensual, passionate woman with needs and desires of her own which will certainly equal and occasionally even outstrip those of her partner. Five is the number of pure and simple sexuality and if anyone cries off with a headache in this partnership it's most likely going to be Mr Three because Miss Five can sometimes be more than any man can cope with. And he had better not turn her down too often or she will soon become irritable, bad-tempered and eventually decide to seek her pleasures elsewhere. Mr Three is going to need plenty of stamina in this relationship because the minute he shows signs of weakening he is going to lose.

Male Three:Female Six

Mr Three and Miss Six should get on famously together because their personalities are very similar and completely in tune. When they finally decide to put down roots this will be a partnership which can withstand almost anything that life chooses to throw at it. However, nothing short of marriage will do for Miss Six. She's far too conventional and idealistic to cope with co-habitation. It has to be all or nothing where she's concerned, so Mr Three's intentions had better be honourable because this woman demands total commitment.

Mr Three is an ambitious man; he wants to rise in the world and can never be truly satisfied in a subordinate position. He needs to have authority and is shrewd, observant and versatile enough to achieve his ends. What's more, he is an incredibly lucky person and even apparent misfortunes have a way of turning out well for him in the long run. Then along comes Miss Six to complete the picture for him. Almost overnight he becomes the well-balanced, wholesome, respectable family man that employers tend to favour. How can he fail to get on with a woman like her at his side?

Miss Six is loyal, faithful and loving, in fact she's the perfect wife and mother. A brilliant career of her own means nothing to her. But don't go thinking she's dull and boring! Miss Six is an intelligent, creative person in her own right and certainly a very great asset to Mr Three. She's an excellent cook, a born hostess and when it comes to entertaining clients in a lavish manner at home and on a low budget, few women can equal her. What's more she is interesting company, a good judge of character and utterly charming. He can hardly fail to clinch a deal once his unsuspecting victims have sampled her hospitality. They make an excellent team because they are united in their efforts.

In any relationship, however well matched, there is always room for improvement and this 3:6 combination is no exception. Mr Three can be obstinate at times and he should always think twice before he decides to start laying down the law because Miss Six can be a very determined character. Once she has dug in her heels over something nothing short of an earthquake will move her. Mr Three must learn to be less wasteful when teamed with an economical woman like this if he wants to avoid trouble because she simply can't bear to throw anything away which might possibly come in handy at some later date.

Miss Six also has a few minor adjustments to make. She needs to curb her tendency to make others emotionally dependent upon her. And she should try not to be quite so fussy about minor details because nothing can ever be perfect in this life, not even for her. Finally she should come to terms with the fact that he will always win in a battle of wits and realize that her sarcasm won't help matters. It will only serve to spur him on and make her even more angry in the long run.

The intimate side of this 3:6 liaison is the only area which is likely to prove disappointing and then perhaps only for Mr Three — because Miss Six is not a particularly sensual woman. She is motherly rather than sexual and although capable of great depth of feeling she is neither passionate nor demonstrative by nature. Mr Three, on the other hand, is an active man of the world and Miss Six may have to turn a blind eye to some of his extramarital activities if she can't manage to fulfil all his needs. But she'll probably be quite willing to do so, as long as she feels that the basis of their love is maintained.

Male Three:Female Seven

On the face of it this seems rather a strange combination but it is one which can work reasonably well at a personal level if both partners are prepared to play by the rules. Mr Three is an easy-going man who can adapt to fit in with most circumstances. He is bold, lively and very charming. In fact he's the complete opposite of the quiet, introverted Miss Seven. He is extremely intelligent, has a brilliant mind and is creative, imaginative, original and intuitive. Mr Three's ideas are novel, he doesn't mince words and, what's more, he's also artistic. These are the attributes she admires and which draw her to him, because she needs a partner with brains who can understand her strange philosophies and appreciate what she's striving to achieve. A man who won't take time off occasionally to dream and fantasize is no good to her. She is a spiritual person and Mr Three is sufficiently enlightened to be able to bring out the best provided he doesn't push too hard.

He should try not to pressurize her too much; she moves at a slower pace than him. She needs to spend some time on her own to study and meditate so he should be sympathetic and give her room to breathe. Most important, he must always take what she says seriously especially when she's trying to explain a particularly profound theory to him. He can be very flippant at times and nothing will alienate her feelings quicker than the thought that he is mocking her and making fun of her beliefs. And there will be many times when he will have to keep a very straight face indeed at some of her ideas.

And what's so special about Miss Seven; why does he choose her when he can have his pick of other women? The answer is quite simple — she's different, she's an enigma and she makes him think, which is just what he needs. Pretty, decorative woman are all very well but he soon gets bored with them, but Miss Seven is studious, intellectual, well-read and really rather mysterious. She's a worthy adversary, offers a constant challenge and makes his imagination work overtime.

This gifted, unusual, magical and secretive woman has three regulations to remember in order to keep this 3:7 relationship running smoothly. She must learn to be more practical and realistic. And she will need to be more careful with money. Finally she must be prepared to socialize and entertain. Mr Three likes company, has many friends and won't want to spend all his spare time in deep and earnest discussion with her. He has so much to offer and the give and take should be in balanced proportions for a happy partnership.

Surprisingly the mystical Miss Seven is very earthy and not at all ethereal when it comes to the physical expression of her love for Mr Three. Here she becomes a different person preferring actions to words every time. She's sensual, emotional, demonstrative and highly imaginative. He is also passionate and exciting and together they should experience the true meaning of the word ecstasy. There should be no complaints, only the satisfied smiles of two blissfully happy, contented lovers.

Male Three:Female Eight

Unfortunately this combination doesn't work well on a personal level. Three and Eight are conflicting numbers (one odd, one even) and when such a combination occurs there are usually very marked differences of opinion and frequent clashes of personality. Mr Three's lesson in life is 'to be able to express himself freely' while Miss Eight's is 'to be materially successful and have authority'. So when these two strong, forceful characters come together under the same roof it requires not only a superhuman effort but also tremendous self-control from both to make the relationship work.

Mr Three is ambitious but he's also easy-going and can never really take things seriously. Miss Eight, on the other hand, is equally ambitious but she's utterly ruthless in those pursuits. She won't be at all amused when he teases her about her career or fails to take advantage of an opportunity for advancement simply because he cannot be bothered to make the effort. She wishes he would specialize more and really develop his creative potential instead of being such a Jack of all trades. Money means everything to her and he could do much better if he really tried. But he won't.

Mr Three doesn't like routine. He's changeable, impulsive, extravagant, obstinate, hates to be in a subordinate position, chafes under the least restraint, dislikes being under an obligation to others and trusts far too much to luck. What is she going to do with him? Why can't he follow her example and really make something of himself? He's totally infuriating but somehow she can't help loving him because, for all his faults, he has a fine brain, he's great company and is utterly charming. She finds him irresistible and irritating all at once.

Miss Eight is quite a different kettle of fish. Her values in life are purely material. She judges everyone by what they have achieved and never bothers to find out who they really are or what they're like. She is strong, tough, practical and, at times, hard and selfish. Any woman who possesses these qualities tends to demand far more from her partner than he can actually provide. Unless she plays down this aggressive, grasping attitude it could do incalculable damage to her relationship with Mr Three. Few men can stand an avaricious, social-climbing woman, however attractive, for too long.

Even the intimate side of this relationship is fraught with dangers, few of them of Mr Three's making. He's loyal, warm and affectionate, never possessive and seldom jealous. He is exciting, imaginative, versatile and caring and a thoughtful lover who can only feel fulfilled when his partner is eager and responsive to his advances. He could encounter a great many problems with Miss Eight because hers is a number of extremes and her moods can swing from gentle and sympathetic one minute to brusque and detached the next. She is on an emotional see-saw and his timing will have to be just right for their lovemaking.

Male Three:Female Nine

An extremely compatible combination — when these two join forces they have everything to gain and nothing at all to lose.

Three is the number of enlightenment and those ruled by it are sympathetic and understanding. Mr Three is creative, artistic and refined. He is talented, witty, imaginative and versatile. He has a brilliant mind, an abundance of original ideas and a certain charm which Miss Nine could hardly fail to fall for. He is generous and impulsive, always full of surprises and always interested in what his partner is doing and how she feels. He is happy, easy-going, not particularly interested in money and ever ready to compromise if its means a speedy end to a disagreement. He's the sort of man that Miss Nine immediately likes. She is usually a very good judge of character and is unlikely to have made a mistake over Mr Three.

Miss Nine is honest, trusting and loyal. She too knows how to compromise with humour and can even disagree without rancour. Like him, she has a clear, quick mind, a good imagination, a fine command or words and that same impulsive streak which can get them both into trouble on occasions. She is determined, active, courageous and a fighter. She is resourceful, inspiring, stimulating, influential and the perfect partner for Mr Three with her wide sympathies and broad-minded attitude. Miss Nine is patient and never gives in. Together they make quite a team.

Mr Three can be outspoken at times but his partner has a thick skin and won't let that worry her. He can be obstinate but she has a way of dealing with that. And if he gets too bossy then she's just the woman to put him firmly, but tactfully, in his place. They couldn't really fall out if they tried because she's not particularly argumentative and he's much too fond of her ever to want to upset her feelings. This relationship seems almost too good to be true but it's a numerological fact that once this 3:9 combination becomes established both parties are usually extremely happy and tend to remain so for the rest of their lives.

The private side of their life together is really the final accolade — the jewel in the crown of an already perfect relationship. Mr Three is kind, loving and affectionate. He cares very deeply for Miss Nine and this is reflected in his lovemaking which is tender and warm. And her feelings certainly match his; she is a romantic, passionate woman; always ready to respond to his advances and certainly not afraid to make a few of her own when the mood takes her. They should experience great physical joy together and even greater pain if they ever have to be apart. This is a relationship in a million.

Male Four:Female One

Mr Four and Miss One will have a long, uphill struggle ahead of them. They're on totally different wavelengths and it will take a monumental effort if this combination is to succeed at all.

Mr Four is a model citizen — he is solid, practical, reliable, and extremely respectable as well as being highly respected by his employers. What on earth is he doing getting mixed up with a domineering, impatient woman like Miss One? She is definitely not his type and they don't even seem to have anything very much in common except perhaps their mutual capacity for hard work. Mr Four is the archetypal model husband. He's efficient, organized and makes a wonderful administrator. He handles money carefully, is utterly trustworthy and is, at heart, a homeloving, family man who attaches great importance to this area of his life. He's not particularly ambitious and is at his happiest when working for someone else. In fact he is really far too dull and boring for Miss One. There is not enough life in him to keep her amused for long. As for his spirit of adventure — it's non-existent! He will probably never understand her behaviour and it's most out of character for him even to want to try.

Miss One is an ambitious, career-minded lady who really doesn't want to be bothered with anything quite so mundane and time-consuming as raising a family and keeping house. But if she must, then she would rather continue going out to work in order to pay someone else to attend to all those trivial, tedious duties on her behalf. She is vital, energetic, courageous and will overcome any obstacle or endure any hardship without complaint, simply to achieve her goal. She is intelligent, self-reliant, tenacious and independent. In an emergency she can always be relied upon to do what has to be done calmly and resolutely, because she is a born leader and is always in complete control.

She craves power and influence and can be extremely aggressive, obstinate and downright tyrannical when the mood takes her. Why she is even remotely attracted to Mr Four will always be an enigma although he does represent security and stability which are both desirable characteristics and he could be a very steadying influence upon her, if only she'd listen to him. Because she needs to make progress in her life at the expense of everything else she will soon tire of his predictable ways and set her sights on someone or something new which offers a greater challenge to her pioneering soul.

Miss One is a busy woman so private moments of intimacy would have to be fitted in between her numerous other social and business commitments. Mr Four is kind, considerate and sensitive. He will do anything in his power to make the women he loves happy but, perhaps, he is not quite powerful and passionate enough to amuse this particular 'One' for long. She needs a strong, ardent partner with plenty of life in him. Miss One is adventurous, athletic and certainly not afraid to reverse roles or take the initiative when she's feeling particularly lively. She could be rather too liberated for his liking. He wants to be loved, not intimidated, and she wants a man, not a mouse, to share her bed.

Male Four: Female Two

Four and Two are both 'even' numbers and this combination points to a harmonious coexistence. Both partners will have special qualities to contribute and will tend to bring out the best, rather than the worst, in each other. They also come under the heading of 'Business Numbers' which means both parties are stable, efficient and well-organized individuals.

Mr Four represents everything Miss Two could ever hope to find in a man. He knows how to build a life around them and she instinctively knows what's required of her to keep things running smoothly. They complement each other perfectly and the possibility of disagreements between them is remote. He is honest, respectable and solid. He offers the security and stability she so desperately craves. She needs someone steady to lean on and he's just the man for the job because he is utterly dependable. Mr Four is calm, practical, very down-to-earth and extremely well-organized. His heart is always where his wife and family are and he's a patriotic, home-loving, sentimental, ideal husband. He's careful with money but exceptionally generous to the woman he loves. He will make any sacrifice for her and asks nothing more than to be loved in return. He is diplomatic, thoughtful, dislikes quarrels and will always make every effort to get along with his in-laws. Miss Two couldn't possibly ask for anything more and she certainly won't need to with Mr Four as her man.

There is nothing aggressive or grasping about Miss Two, in fact she's quite the opposite — shy, sweet-natured and rather self-conscious — and that's just what Mr Four likes about her. He knows where he stands with this woman and he treasures peace and quiet almost as much as she does. She is even-tempered, kind and friendly. She has a superb imagination, is creative, sensitive and deeply intuitive. Her conversation is interesting, her humour surprisingly sharp and her judgement well balanced. However, like the moon, she does have a darker side to her nature which can cause problems in any relationship. Her moods and emotions are very changeable, she's almost incapable of making a decision because she keeps changing her mind and finally she tends to be jealous and possessive. Mr Four can also be suspicious and inclined to get despondent. They will both need to tread with care in this area of their relationship.

When it comes to the intimate side of their relationship, Mr Four and Miss Two should experience great personal joy although they will never taste the extremes of sheer animal passion because they are both too modest and conventional. Mr Four is a tender, loving man, always full of consideration for his partner and far too conformist to suggest they might try sexual experiments. And Miss Two expresses her love for him in a gentle, romantic way because even when they're alone she still tends to be very timid and inhibited. But neither will seem disappointed with their lovemaking, because the way they choose to express their emotions seems to be just right.

Male Four:Female Three

Unless these two can manage to overcome their personality differences, this relationship isn't going to be easy — in fact a break is always possible.

Mr Four likes things just the way they are and doesn't want to change. He is solid, down-to-earth and immovable. Miss Three, on the other hand, sails through life being bold, imaginative, versatile and very impulsive.

Mr Four is a builder. He constructs his life slowly and with the utmost care, one brick at a time and then only when he's satisfied that his foundations are as strong and durable as they possibly can be. He is methodical, industrious, stolid and calm. Nothing ever seems to shake him and he rarely gives up even when the going gets difficult. He won't cut corners and he never takes risks however hard he may be pushed. Like 'Ole Man River' Mr Four just keeps rolling along. People tend to regard him as a dull, joyless person but on closer inspection they soon discover that he has a fine, inventive mind, interesting conversation and plenty of amusing stories to recount.

The other half of the combination, Miss Three, can certainly be summed up by the way she looks. She has a merry twinkle in her eye which says she is lively and full of fun, a spring in her walk which indicates she is ready for anything and a way of looking at people which tells them she is shrewd, observant and bright. She does, in fact, have a very agile brain which she is not afraid to use. She is imaginative, inventive, creative and intuitive. Unfortunately, she's also rather inclined to be frivolous. Not only does she act without thought but she also calls a spade a spade and her direct, tactless manner of speech often gives offence even though none is intended. She is an easy-going, friendly woman who could be utterly charming with the addition of just a little more self-discipline and restraint.

The private side of this relationship certainly rests on the strongest foundation stone of all — love. Despite their undeniable differences these two are very fond of each other which becomes evident in an intimate environment. Mr Four is a sentimental man. He is kind, considerate, faithful and devoted. He is also surprisingly sensitive and needs to feel loved and emotionally secure in his personal life. He is capable of great depths of feeling although rarely possessive or jealous and fortunately neither is Miss Three. She is loyal, warm and caring. Her impulsive streak is still in evidence but in the privacy of their own room it becomes a source of amusement rather than irritation, because Mr Four never knows what she's going to do next. Even if they do hit a good many lows in this relationship, the high notes that they reach should more than compensate for the problems they might encounter in their daily lives.

Male Four:Female Four

These two might well start off their life together like any other pair of starry-eyed lovers but, by the time they've finished, their little love-nest will probably have grown into a sumptuous, fairy-tale palace with all the latest labour-saving devices. Why? — because four is the number of 'foundation', so a pair of Fours will build bigger and better than anyone else. The need to construct something durable and permanent is in their blood and although they may not work at great speed the final result will be quite spectacular. These two are the proverbial 'Jones's' that everyone else is trying to 'keep up with'. However, there is one great danger to guard against when two Fours join forces; they could become so materially minded that they allow other vital aspects of life to pass them by.

Mr Four is efficient, superbly well-organized and certainly not afraid of hard work. He is practical, down-to-earth and can be relied upon for his calm, steady approach to any problem. He excels at systemization which is why he can get through a heavy workload with apparent ease. He has a brilliant, inventive mind, plenty to say for himself and a way of attracting people without being pushy or aggressive. He tends to view everything from a different angle to others and usually sides with the underdog in any dispute. Whatever he achieves in life you can be sure he has worked very hard for it; he's utterly trustworthy, never takes short cuts to get something done and handles money with care and respect, which is probably why he seems to be able to make his finances go much further than anyone else. He is a respectable, respected, homeloving family man. He does suffer from gloomy bouts of melancholy occasionally but they rarely last for long and are seldom severe enough to merit the description 'depressions'. He's solid, reliable, industrious and the perfect companion for another of his own kind — Miss Four.

The female of this species has exactly the same nature as her male counterpart. She's well-organized and runs her home and family to perfection. She needs to feel safe and secure at all times and for this reason Mr Four is the ideal husband for her. Her home is of great importance as it represents an excellent outlet for her organizational talents. In order to be truly happy everything around her has to tick over like well-oiled clockwork.

This pair are not particularly sensual or sexually adventurous but within their relationship there is mutual respect and trust which so often outlives the pleasures of the flesh. Fours are sentimental, faithful and considerate to each other. Neither of them are jealous or possessive and all they ever ask from their private lives is to love and to be loved in return. Anything else is an added bonus.

Male Four:Female Five

Although Mr Four and Miss Five are as different as chalk and cheese, opposites often attract. With a little effort on both sides to get the balance properly adjusted and their undeniable differences ironed out, this unlikely combination can be seen to work well. Mr Four is solid and could do with some of the imagination which Miss Five provides; he's practical, she's adjustable; he's well-organized, she's rather a scatterbrain; he's calm, while she's a fidget. They are a typical example of conflicting numbers (one even, one odd) but in this combination the strong points in each other's basic make-up tend to compensate for weaknesses in their partners. In fact most of the qualities that one lacks the other seems to possess and this provides both parties with ample room to manoeuvre and plenty of scope for expansion.

Good old Mr Four is a real brick. He is dependable, reliable and can offer Miss Five the security which she pretends to scorn in public; but even she secretly needs an anchor in life and a safe harbour in which to weather the storms. Adventures are for the young and only when she grows older will she fully appreciate what a considerate, exceptional man her partner really is. She loves to tease him, especially when he frowns at some of her more madcap schemes. Then she'll playfully accuse him of being a boring old stick-in-the-mud although, without his sensible, down-to-earth influence, who knows what trouble her recklessness could result in.

Mr Four works hard and pays attention to detail. He is patient, persevering and doesn't take unnecessary risks. He never gives up when the going gets difficult and can certainly stare reality squarely in the face without flinching. He is respectable, responsible and very good at making a little go a long way, particularly where money is concerned.

Miss Five has an elastic mind and boundless energy. She is clever, jumpy, impatient and difficult to pin down. She does many things well and her main problem lies in choosing the right objective because she's attracted by everything and held by nothing. That is until Mr Four comes along to provide her with a direction in life. He is one person who can successfully manage to clip her wings but not destroy her spirit. She wants excitement just like others needs peace and quiet. She can be selfish, thoughtless and inconsiderate but in Mr Four's eyes her originality, creativity and perception count for much more. Getting involved with her is perhaps the only gamble he will ever take in his life. Fortunately with a little give and take and a genuine desire to get along this risk should reward them both handsomely because he never gives up and she never knows when to stop.

Any woman who has Mr Four for her partner should count herself lucky. He's full of little treats and surprises. He is kind, loving, sentimental and a man who can offer his love without imposing restrictions. He is big-hearted, generous and simply wants to make his partner happy. He's not particularly passionate or demonstrative but he makes up for this in a host of other ways. And in return for his trust and devotion he asks nothing more than to be loved.

Our Miss Five can be quite a handful for any red-blooded male. She's sensual, earthy and extremely lively. She knows what she wants and if it's not given fast enough she is likely to help herself. Mr Four will need to be on his mettle here although if he can tame her in public the same tactics could also work in private. He should regard her as a time-bomb which needs to be defused although not rendered completely harmless. This could be quite a tricky operation but one which should be very enjoyable (for both parties) to carry out.

Male Four:Female Six

This 4:6 combination has the makings of a very sound personal relationship as it contains all the right ingredients for harmony. Firstly the numbers Four and Six are balanced, even and divisible by two which indicates both parties will have a good deal in common, although Miss Six will have a slightly more complex personality because her number is also divisible by three — this we will analyse later.

Mr Four is an energetic, hard-working idealist. He tends towards practicality and is calm, solid and very down-to-earth in his approach to life. He's a born organizer and for this reason he usually appears to accomplish so much with little effort. He believes that, through logic and good planning, almost anything can be achieved. But despite his steady, respectable appearance there is nothing dull about him. He is stimulating company, a good conversationalist and full of amusing stories. He's patriotic, home-loving and very easy to get along with. However, his feelings are easily wounded, he can be over-sensitive at times and is rather inclined to suffer the odd periodic bouts of the blues when his responsibilities seem a little heavy. He represents safety, security and equilibrium which are all qualities that Miss Six can recognize and to which she can relate.

Miss Six is also reliable, well-balanced, equable and idealistic. She has a positive genius for home and family life and because she is sympathetic and understanding she knows instinctively how to approach Mr Four when he's in a sensitive mood or feeling despondent and rather melancholy. Her goal in life is to give help and support when it's needed although she will occasionally take this to extremes. Generally she is warm-hearted, honest, loyal and very conventional. She has charm, dignity and a strong sense of decency. Once she has chosen a partner she becomes deeply attached to him. He is the most important thing in her life, together with her children if she has any. Nothing is too much trouble for her, she will go to great lengths to avoid an argument but should that happen she will always be the first to apologize and make amends. Hers is the number of peace, harmony and domesticity and that is what she strives to achieve at all times. The complexity of her character which was mentioned earlier manifests itself in her artistic talents. She is creative, imaginative and has an eye for colour. And she's such a well-adjusted person that her talents serve to enhance not only her personality but her home as well. Although Mr Four does not share her creative ability he can nevertheless appreciate her efforts.

The peace and harmony that already exists between this couple should spill over into their moments of intimacy and while their lovemaking may never have that feeling of urgency about it, generosity and consideration will certainly abound. Mr Four is really an old softie because he's sentimental, romantic and tender while his partner, Miss Six, is loyal, faithful and warmly affectionate. When this combination occurs in a personal relationship it promises happiness and fulfilment for both participants.

Male Four: Female Seven

This combination promises great happiness for all concerned because it is balanced by the best characteristics of both worlds. Mr Four represents the material plane providing the solid foundations for their relationship to rest upon while Miss Seven, who is a very spiritual person, contributes creativity, imagination and a certain dream-like quality which her down-to-earth partner lacks. Together they have great potential and the keyword for this particular union can only be 'expansion'.

Mr Four has a very distinct character. He is hard-working, energetic, solid, practical and well-balanced. He's also patient, persevering, respectable and acts as an anchor for the relationship. He never indulges in flights of fancy and is a calming, sobering influence when Miss Seven's intuitive powers carry her beyond the bounds of reason. He is intelligent, inventive, home-loving and good at handling money, which is just as well because Miss Seven is hopeless at finances.

While Mr Four may be efficient and organized he does like to question authority, always takes a different view of matters presented to him and often holds very positive and unconventional views and opinions. He and his partner are seldom at a loss for topics of discussion.

He brings security, steadiness and equilibrium to their relationship. In return he gains truth and wisdom because Miss Seven can reach his soul. She's his guru, his own private window onto other worlds which they can explore quietly together in the peaceful surroundings of their own home.

Seven is the magic number and Miss Seven is positively magical and mysterious. She is intellectual, philosophical, self-controlled and rather secretive which could irritate Mr Four at first until he gets to know her better. She's studious, reserved, interested in the occult and probably also gifted with powers of ESP, perhaps in the form of clairvoyance or clairaudience. She is dignified rather than charming and money and physical comforts offer little importance to her. But she does need to spend some time completely on her own in order to think, meditate and study. She is quite a puzzle and one which Mr Four may never solve although his attempts to unravel her mysteries should be interesting, rewarding and will last him a lifetime.

Intimacy for these two is a union of minds as well as bodies. They could reach heights of sheer ecstasy never achieved by other couples simply because they're completely in tune with each other on all levels or 'planes of experience'. Mr Four is considerate, kind, caring and, strangely enough in such a stolid man, extremely sentimental and romantic. Miss Seven is emotional and passionate but always manages to keep her feelings well under control. There are times when he wonders if her thoughts are really with him or whether she has allowed them to drift away on some strange fantasy or other, but he never bothers to ask because it's not that important. What does matter is that they are together and that's how they are likely to remain.

Male Four:Female Eight

'Business and pleasure' — that sums up a 4:8 combination. This couple could either be colleagues, for whom a close personal relationship develops outside office hours, or they will meet socially and later decide to go into partnership. But no matter how they get together one thing is certain, the chances are they will eventually live and work together. The urge to make money is in their blood and with its double-helping of drive, efficiency and ambition this combination can hardly fail to reach its goal.

Let us look at Miss Eight first because she's the real power behind the throne and the driving force in the relationship. She sees everything on a very large scale and will never be satisfied until they have built a small empire for themselves and have managed to achieve not only material success but also social standing. Miss Eight can be hard and utterly ruthless when necessary. She knows how to use her strength, practical abilities and energy in a creative way and if anyone deserves a medal for sheer tenacity and concentrated effort then it has to be her. She is adaptable, reliable, responsible and charming. As the dominant character in this relationship she needs to guard against obstinacy, selfishness and aggression as these are all qualities which do nothing to enhance her personality. She also regards a certain amount of quarrelling as normal which Mr Four could find very wearing at times. She wants comfort, luxury and a grand lifestyle and somehow she'll bully, nag, charm and cajole him into getting it for them. She is the lion in this relationship and sadly he will always be the expendable lamb who can be sacrificed at any time. Don't ever let Miss Eight fool you into thinking she's only a playful pussycat; this woman means business; nothing and no one will be allowed to stand in her way for long.

Mr Four doesn't think on such a grand scale as his partner but this can be helpful because he should be able to pinpoint and correct minor problems before they get out of hand and damage her overall scheme. He is not as dynamic or aggressive as Miss Eight although he can be just as obstinate and determined. He's practical, hard-working and, like her, very good at handling money but he is rather more down-to-earth in his approach to life and doesn't expect the same enormous rewards for his endeavours. He is calm, efficient, very organized and an excellent administrator, which fits in nicely with her plans for them both. Together they could move mountains, provided Miss Eight doesn't push Mr Four too hard.

Eight represents reversals which means that a great success can become a spectacular failure. So while this relationship could prosper things could also go very wrong between them and it's anyone's guess whether it will last for four or forty years.

Unfortunately moments of intimacy for this couple are likely to be fairly few and far between because Miss Eight is subject to great extremes of emotion and often shows little interest in the physical side of love. Occasionally she can be gentle and sympathetic but most of the time she's rather cool and detached in private because she has difficulty in expressing her affections. Mr Four is a considerate man but he's only human and his feelings are easily hurt. Once he realizes that his advances are not always welcome he will probably give up altogether and decide to read a book instead. This area of their relationship might always be a problem.

Male Four:Female Nine

Mr Four and Miss Nine constitute a walking disaster area if they should combine forces in the hard, ruthless world of commerce but when they come together in a personal relationship it's another story altogether. They have much to teach one another and the learning process is necessarily slow if information is to be properly absorbed and fully understood. Mr Four has practical skills to pass on to his partner and, in turn, Miss Nine is inspiring, stimulating and very well informed. It's her worldly wisdom which she imparts to her mate. If this relationship is allowed to develop at its own pace it should go from strength to strength.

Mr Four is probably the best teacher Miss Nine could ever have. He is patient, persevering, pays attention to detail and knows his subject well. His pupil is intelligent, interested and eager to learn which means that they set off on a very good footing. He is a calm person who thinks before he acts whereas Miss Nine is rather excitable and impulsive, so he can teach her how to control her enthusiasm and hopefully make fewer mistakes. By copying the steady, responsible example he sets she will discover how a down-to-earth attitude can work wonders at times and, by facing up to reality, problems can be viewed in perspective. This is only a fraction of what he has to offer her and every day in his company will bring fresh discoveries.

And what of Miss Nine? She can teach her partner the right way to live through her breadth of thinking. She's compassionate, understanding, idealistic and, like Mr Four, also very patient. She has wide sympathies and tremendous charm. She is capable of exerting great influence not only over other people but also her whole environment. She has a strong will, a clear, quick mind, the occasional unpredictable flash of inspiration and a genuine desire to make the world a better place to live in. Mr Four is putty in her hands and she will soon have him at her side waging war against hunger, poverty and political oppression. She is a talented, clever woman who by helping him develop a broad-minded attitude to life will be fulfilling the life mission of a Number Nine which is to promote universal love and harmony.

In the privacy of their own bedroom these two can still teach each other a thing or two. Mr Four brings romance, sentiment and consideration to their lovemaking while she is impulsive, unselfish and demonstrative. His gentleness seems to balance, and sometimes even outweighs, her haste and together they should experience great joy and happiness which only true love and deep affection can bring to a relationship.

Male Five:Female One

Stand well back when Mr Five and Miss One leave the starting grid and take the road together in a Grand Prix personal relationship. Fortunately both drivers are extremely adaptable and versatile and this could be the saving grace in a 5:1 combination. They're both very changeable individuals who need to adapt quickly and readily to cope with each other's demands.

Mr Five is best described as a fidget. He's restless, impatient and highly-strung. He never takes proper care of himself, lives on his nerves, burns the candle at both ends, runs the most fearful risks and eventually his mental batteries are so low that he becomes prey to nervous disorders of the worst kind. Even under slight pressure he can become irritable and quick-tempered. What he needs is a woman who will mother him but Miss One certainly won't do that. She takes the attitude that if he doesn't abide by the elementary rules like eating properly, getting enough sleep and so on, then he should be scratched from the race. She lives by the laws of the jungle where only the fittest survive.

But Mr Five does have many good points which counterbalance his short-comings. He's extremely astute, a good organizer and a wise delegator. Nothing seems to get him down for long and he manages to rebound quickly from even the heaviest blow. He's adventurous, attractive and craves nothing more than excitement. Anything else, such as financial gain or social status, which he may achieve in the course of his eventful life, are mere incidentals because he seeks thrills rather than rewards.

The ambitious, aggressive Miss One brings out the best and the worst in Mr Five at one and the same time. This relationship may not stand the test of time but it will certainly be fun while it lasts with two such active, dynamic partners battling it out for first place. They present the perfect picture of 'one-upmanship' — both trying to outdo and outdare the other at all times. But Miss One is likely to emerge wearing the winner's laurel because she has the staying power and determination which Mr Five lacks. He is rather inclined to give up when the going gets tough although he could well decide to have a second try at taming this woman at a later date.

Miss One is a career woman. She likes to get her own way and is afraid of nothing. She is single-minded, positive, courageous and self-contained. She has a pioneering spirit and is usually drawn to the new and unusual which is also a characteristic she shares with her partner. She is intelligent, logical, creative and tenacious but unfortunately also obstinate, aggressive and terribly bossy.

Both can be an embarrassment to their family and friends at times as they don't seem to require privacy when it comes to showing their feelings about each other. They are demonstrative, extrovert and impulsive. When they're finally tucked up behind locked doors, it's a case of anything goes. Miss One treats lovemaking in exactly the same way as she does everything else in life which means that once she has made up her mind, nothing will stop her. And her partner is no better (or worse). Five is the number of the natural man, the sensualist, and Mr Five certainly tries to live up to expectations.

Male Five:Female Two

'And never the twain shall meet' or indeed agree about anything in a 5:2 relationship! This is a prime example of conflicting numbers which can be found in Numerology from time to time when two numbers oppose each other. When such a combination exists there are often very marked differences of opinion and frequent clashes of personality between the two in question. Physical attraction is not enough; their difficulties lie in understanding each other's thoughts and motives. Although these tricky combinations can occasionally be made to work — but only with a great deal of effort, understanding and determination — it will probably never make the grade as Mr Five values his freedom too much and Miss Two is far too timid and hesitant ever to put her foot down and make him toe the line.

It seems that Mr Five is usually the main cause of trouble in any relationship. He is clever, resilient and resourceful with a tremendous spirit of adventure, a craving for excitement and nerves as taut as piano wires. And just like a piano he occasionally needs to be re-tuned. He loves to explore new places and investigate new ideas, hates getting into a rut and thrives on danger, risk and, sometimes, gambling. He is talented and can do many things passibly well but tends to be attracted to everything and held by nothing for very long. Miss Two could very soon discover this when he starts to cast his eyes in the direction of other women; some of whom may be her closest friends. Miss Two might be better off without him although he does have a certain charm which is hard to resist. She will probably learn her lesson the hard way in this relationship; but it's one mistake she probably won't make again.

Miss Two is one of life's innocents. She is submissive, modest, sensitive and reserved. She's rather shy, terribly self-conscious, changes her mind frequently and is extremely indecisive because she is so easily influenced. She is creative, superbly imaginative, generous, friendly and far too good for an incorrigible rogue like Mr Five. She loves beauty, harmony and order so she is in for a rude awakening when this untidy, restless, noisy man bursts into her life changing everything around and then departing in the same whirlwind haste in which he arrived. Miss Two is emotional, gentle, moody, easily hurt and often deeply wounded by the slightest criticism or harsh remark. It could take her a considerable time to recover from the ravages of Mr Five.

Even the initial physical attraction is sometimes not enough to keep these two together as they both have entirely different views about love and the way it is expressed. Miss Two is all hearts and flowers. She's tender, romantic and dreamy whereas Mr Five is sensual, sexy and spontaneous. His lovemaking is often raw, animal and unorthodox. He'll never write sentimental verse in praise of her beauty and purity any more than she will ever be able to play him at his own game.

Male Five: Female Three

The restless swallow (Mr Five) and the versatile otter (Miss Three) are a lively and very striking twosome. They are both active, creative extroverts with adaptable natures and fine brains and they truly believe that life is for living. The only danger lies in overhastiness, which is something they will always have to guard against.

When two numbers are both odd it implies that the relationship should be reasonably harmonious because both will have unique qualities to contribute which bring out the best, rather than the worst, in each other. Let's see how this works in real life.

Mr Five is a restless individual. He needs constant stimulation to keep him from getting into a rut. Unfortunately he also loses interest very quickly and once he has become bored he soon starts casting around for something different to try. This is where Miss Three can help because she is clever, resourceful and full of bright ideas. If she can't keep him amused then no one can. Mr Five is an adventure seeker, he loves to travel, meet new people and explore different surroundings. He needs to be on the go all the time and if there is an element of risk involved then so much the better because he is one of life's gamblers. Again Miss Three can prove indispensable here as she seems to have the luck of the Devil; with her beside him he simply can't go wrong. Even when he's tired and irritable (as he frequently seems to be from living on his nerves too much) it doesn't bother her at all. She can't take his grumpiness seriously and, what's more, she knows that after a good night's sleep he will wake up in the morning his usual unpredictable, impatient self. 'How on earth do you put up with him?' her friends often ask in amazement when he has done something particularly bizarre or thoughtless and her answer is always the same, 'Because there's something different about him which keeps me on my toes'. It goes without saying that she loves the old fidget as well!

Miss Three is quite an unusual lady. She is highly talented, especially in the arts, decidedly ambitious, independent and versatile. Mr Five shares her artistic leanings and his criticisms can be extremely constructive and helpful at times even though she does tend to fly off the handle if she doesn't agree with some of them. Her speech can often be too direct: she always says exactly what she feels no matter who it offends. Not only is she gifted, she's also shrewd, observant and generally one step ahead of everyone else. She's satirical, thinks at great speed and takes a secret delight in running rings around those with slower minds than herself. Mr Five's mind is certainly not slow and he gives her a good run for her money although she usually emerges triumphant in the end.

These two have similar paths to tread through life which is probably why they seem to get along so well together. He needs to be progressive and experience as much as possible while she must take opportunities to develop her potential whenever they arise. Even their life lessons are almost, but not quite, the same. He has to learn the right way to use freedom and she must learn to express herself freely.

One area which needs little excavation is their private life. It is quite evident from the happy, satisfied looks on both their faces that there are no problems here. Mr Five's number may stand for sexuality but Miss Three can be equally exciting, unpredictable and sensual. He may think of himself as Superman but there's only one character she can possibly be — Wonderwoman. Let's hope they never have occasion to share a telephone kiosk!

Male Five:Female Four

With Mr Five and Miss Four there is a great deal of truth in the old saying 'where there's a will there's a way' because this combination can work moderately well but it will need considerable effort from both parties.

The main stumbling block is their entirely different personalities. Here we have another example of conflicting numbers (one odd, one even), while Five is also a 'mind number' (a thinker) and Four is a 'business number' (a doer). However, opposites often attract and that's possibly what has happened here. Mr Five is imaginative and adjustable, Miss Four is solid and practical; provided they both tread carefully this relationship might make the grade.

Mr Five finds it almost impossible to practice caution. He is a restless, impatient man who is very difficult to pin down and very hard to define as he never heads in the same direction for more than five minutes at a time. He's highly strung, lives on his nerves, is quick in thought and decision and impulsive in his actions, which Miss Four rarely is. He is an adventurer, loves to travel and is stimulated by meeting new people or exploring strange places. He is many-faceted and his greatest difficulty lies in deciding what to do. He find everything attractive although his interest is seldom held by anything for long. He craves excitement, enjoys gambling and sometimes takes the most fearful risks. He is buoyant and resilient. His brain appears to be made from elastic because it will stretch in any direction he chooses. On the negative side, he is so self-reliant that he doesn't really need anyone to advise or encourage him which means that he can be selfish, thoughtless and inconsiderate at times. In general terms he is a charming, attractive but totally unreliable man. It's usually quicker and easier to do things for yourself than to ask for his help. He will either completely forget what he was supposed to be doing for you or else he will come to a grinding halt half way through, when something else takes his fancy.

Fortunately Miss Four is an exceptionally calm, practical, down-to-earth woman who could teach him a thing or two about organization and common sense. She is hard-working, efficient and dependable. She certainly makes up for a great many of his shortcomings although she will soon tire of clearing up his mess, sorting out his problems and having to take all the responsibility. She needs good, solid foundations upon which to build her life, while he rarely gives the cement time to dry before some new fancy takes him off course yet again. This relationship requires effort to make it work and as usual, Mr Five will have to make the largest contribution.

Mr Five is a lusty, red-blooded male so when he finds himself emotionally involved with Miss Four he will have to keep a tight rein on some of his baser instincts if he doesn't want to frighten her away. He is sensual, demonstrative, adventurous and maybe a little too sexy for a conservative lady. Miss Four is kind, loving and considerate but she probably lacks the animal undertones which her partner brings to their lovemaking. Sometimes she can be too self-disciplined for her own good. If he can learn to keep his passion in check and if she becomes less predictable and rather more adventurous this combination stands a fighting chance of pulling through.

Male Five:Female Five

This is a volatile combination from whichever angle you choose to view it. All Fives are restless, changeable, highly strung and rebellious. Put two Fives together and you create a potential time-bomb which is set to go off at any moment. A relationship which involves two Fives is fraught with danger and should, if at all possible, be avoided.

Male Five:Female Six

When the temperamental, excitable Mr Five gets emotionally involved with a quiet, homeloving woman like Miss Six the result can turn out a pleasant surprise for his family and friends who have all begun to despair of him ever settling down. In fact, Miss Six has such a calming influence on him that, for once in his life, he begins to put his thoughts into order.

Mr Five, when left to his own devices, always experiences difficulty in finding a goal simply because he can do so many things well and there are so many things he wants to do. He is also inclined to lose interest in a project after only a short while and decide to try his hand at something else. He lacks staying power and tends to give in to temptation without even a struggle. He is highly strung, restless, impatient, mentally and physically adventurous and exceedingly difficult to pin down. He enjoys gambling, taking risks, travel, meeting new people and exploring exotic places. He is a clever, resourceful man as Miss Six is only too well aware — but she'll see that his talents don't go to waste! He may only be a Jack of all Trades when they first meet, but by the time she's finished with him, he'll be a master craftsman with a great deal of fine work to his credit.

Miss Six is a superb judge of character so she can often see potential in Mr Five that other women overlook. She believes he is worthwhile. She's adept at manipulating people without appearing to have done so because she possesses the rare gift of intuitively understanding their needs and difficulties. She is creative, intelligent, well-balanced, conventional, courageous, determined and supportive. She has an eye for beauty, an excellent colour sense and artistic ability.

Even the symbols for this 5:6 combination, which are both birds, are compatible and this is most encouraging. Miss Six's dove represents peacemaking and generosity while Mr Five's swallow always returns to its nesting place, no matter how far it may have chosen to travel. This means that she will never try to take away his freedom but will welcome him with open arms and never a word of rebuke whenever he returns. She is a rare woman because she can accept and come to terms with his restlessness without animosity or bitterness.

Life is seldom perfect for anyone and the nuptial couch could be where this couple's problems lie. Miss Six's love is more maternal than sensual. Loyal, faithful and romantic she may be, but a fiery temptress she most certainly is not. She knows very well how to comfort and care but she is not cut out for moments of grand passion or animal savagery. Unfortunately, he is and this is where the trouble could start. Five is the number of sexuality and Mr Five likes to live up to his number whenever he can. Miss Six really has only two options open to her; she will either have to accept him as her teacher, and do plenty of homework on the subject, or she will have to turn a blind eye to the risk of extramarital activities.

Male Five:Female Seven

A see-saw is the image which springs to mind for this combination, with

Mr Five sitting confidently at one end and Miss Seven precariously perched at the other. When he's up, she's down and when she's happy, he's not. But there's something very important about a see-saw; when it's completely level it reaches a point of balance and both riders can momentarily see eye to eye. This same equilibrium can be achieved in a 5:7 relationship through consideration, moderation and a very great deal of patience from both parties. However, just like the see-saw, these two never stay in perfect harmony for long and its seems inevitable that their relationship will suffer more than its fair share of emotional ups and downs.

Mr Five is restless, highly-strung and terribly impatient. He loves travel, meeting new people and exploring strange places. He prefers to gain his knowledge and experience first hand rather than from a text book. He does, however, have one great problem; he's so multi-faceted that he seldom sticks to anything for long. Variety is his spice of life so he'll make sure that he tries everything at least once in his lifetime. He's adventurous, daring, impulsive and utterly charming but he can also be thoughtless, critical and dreadfully conceited when the mood takes him. In fact he does have quite a few drawbacks as Miss Seven will find out when she gets to know him. She's a lady who needs peace, quiet and plenty of time to think and those particular commodities will be in very short supply with Mr Five rampaging about the place.

Our worldly, experienced Mr Five has probably never met a woman like Miss Seven and this is precisely what attracts him to her in the first instance. She doesn't seem to conform to any pattern he can recognize. He decides to get to the bottom of the mystery, but what he doesn't realize is that his quest could take a lifetime.

Miss Seven is an enigma whose variations only serve to make her more desirable in his eyes. She is studious, creative and secretive. She has a powerful, penetrating mind and a superb imagination. She uses her intellect to explore the world about her and is particularly interested in discovering the truths concerning the nature and meaning of existence. She's reserved, dignified and artistic. Her worldly needs are few and modest; money and status are of little importance — but her own faith is. It's likely that her beliefs are unorthodox — in fact, a great many of her ideas seem rather peculiar to most people. One thing she does share with Mr Five is a love of travel. However she prefers to get off the tourist track whenever possible and is certainly not afraid to rough it when necessary. If only the see-saw keeps balanced long enough for these to reach a working compromise the relationship could be a rewarding experience for both of them.

Strangely enough, this couple never experience any real problems in their lovemaking. Miss Seven may be quiet and rather withdrawn in public but in private it's quite a different story. She is emotional, passionate and imaginative. Sexy Mr Five has met his match here and any description of their sexual antics is best left to the imagination.

Male Five:Female Eight

Mr Five and Miss Eight make a winning team. They are a dynamic duo with Miss Eight converting ideas into realities almost as fast as Mr Five can dream them up, and this pace of life can often lead to mistakes unless they are both alert and experienced.

Mr Five is certainly alert. In fact he is perceptive, clever, shrewd and resourceful. He does many things well because he's highly talented so the description 'experienced' will also fit. But he is far too highly-strung, impatient, adventurous and willing to run risks for his own good, and even for the good of this relationship. Apart from being inconsiderate, self-indulgent and totally unpredictable at times, he's an attractive, lively character who simply oozes charm and has a great deal to say for himself.

He is original, creative, recovers quickly from misfortunes and has an agile mind which will stretch in three directions at once and never feel a moment's strain. He has a nose for gambles, one eye ever open to spot new ideas, impeccable taste and an overriding fear of getting himself into a rut. He's progressive, ingenious and, with Miss Eight at his side, virtually unstoppable.

Miss Eight has all her wits about her. She is strong, practical and wise and wants desperately to succeed in everything she does, including her relationship. She is intelligent, strong and tenacious but these qualities sometimes manifest themselves in a negative way when she becomes hard, selfish, aggressive and domineering. Few people are as black as they are painted and usually she is the most charming, attractive woman you could ever hope to meet. She is truthful, reliable, never tries to dodge her responsibilities and is always prepared to make sacrifices for her loved ones. She can be quite a tyrant at times but her heart is in the right place. If the adventurer (Mr Five) and the materialist (Miss Eight) cannot manage to enjoy themselves and somehow profit from their union then something is very wrong indeed.

Unfortunately the fun and games could come to a halt once the bedroom door closes. Five is the number of sexuality but Eight is a number of great reversals. She will usually call the tune where lovemaking is concerned and she may even use the 'headache ploy' or the 'stop it, you'll wake the children' excuse more than most women. But fortunately this story does have a happy ending. When she's in a loving mood then time could stand still for them both and Mr Five will find himself wishing that she felt this way more often.

Male Five:Female Nine

A 5:9 combination is neither very good nor very bad — it tends to take the middle path. Mr Five is often the culprit whenever the relationship runs into trouble because he can be thoughtless and impulsive in his behaviour. But Miss Nine, who was born under the highest vibration of all, can usually manage to exert enough influence over him to stop matters from deteriorating further.

When it comes to scaling the heights, Miss Nine deserves all the credit. A number Nine's goal in life, whether male or female, is to promote love and harmony and to show others the right way to live. Quite naturally she'll attempt to bring Mr Five around to her point of view, although if he falls by the wayside her innate understanding will come to the rescue. Whatever risks he takes and no matter how inconsiderate he is, she will always forgive him and this is exactly why a combination like this will stand the test of time. Miss Nine is an exceptional person and in his heart Mr Five knows it.

Mr Five is first and foremost one of life's adventurers. He hates to get into a rut. He needs variety, stimulation and excitement twenty-four hours a day in order to feel truly fulfilled. He is a clever man — talented, original and creative — but he finds it very difficult to cope with plodding, repetitive work of any kind because he has such a butterfly brain. He's many-faceted, highly-strung, resilient, resourceful and almost impossible to pin down. Not many woman can put up with his ways for long but

Miss Nine is different. She brings out the best in him with apparent ease while he stretches her resources, both mental and physical, to the limits. He is quixotic and very difficult to keep up with but these two should cross the finishing line hand in hand; she won't get left behind for a moment.

Miss Nine is a woman of great vision. She is broad-minded, idealistic and very, very determined. She has great personal charm, wide sympathies and an intense urge to serve mankind in a worthwhile cause. She is destined for success and her achievements are often brilliant. She has a clear, quick mind, great imagination, a trusting nature and an honest, truthful way of dealing with her affairs. Her greatest dangers, just like Mr Five, lie in impulsiveness and foolhardiness. She can also be intolerant and rather prejudiced in her attitudes and opinions. She is resourceful, a good organizer and always prepared to fight for what she wants. Mr Five needs a strong woman by his side and Miss Nine will fit the bill.

In private this visionary (Nine) and adventurous (Five) couple get along reasonably well. Most of the time their desire and appetites will be in tune but inevitably they will also experience moments of great ecstasy as well as nights of total disaster. On the one hand Mr Five is sensual, earthy and impatient while Miss Nine on the other is romantic, passionate and impulsive.

Male Six:Female One

There can be little doubt that this 6:1 relationship will flourish and grow because the pros outweigh the cons all along the line. Mr Six is a man with much to offer his woman in the way of loyalty, affection and love but in return she must ensure that there is always sufficient scope for him to express his creative talents in whatever way he chooses. This could mean anything from a fifteen foot statue of Venus in their back garden to a huge mural running the full length of their hallway. One way or another he has to give rein to his artistic gifts and however much this annoys her, she will just have to learn to live with it.

Although she is a liberated career woman, Miss One must channel all her aggression into her work. A bossy little tyrant is the last person our kindly, equable Mr Six wants to share his life with. He needs peace, harmony and tranquility not rows, arguments and constant strife. How she behaves at work is her business but at home she must calm down and stop shouting.

Mr Six is well-balanced, imaginative, intelligent and faithful. After marriage, and it will have to be marriage with him, he will always prefer his partner's company to that of anyone else. He makes a devoted husband, a conscientious father and a lifelong friend. He has moral and emotional courage, self-control and a positive genius for intuitively understanding the needs and difficulties of others. He likes rich colours and beautiful objects and these tastes are reflected wherever he goes, especially in his own home. He is open-minded, dignified, extremely magnetic and capable of great charm. Like everyone else he does have his occasional 'off-days' when he can be lacklustre, self-indulgent or even downright obstinate and unyielding. He is a man you can trust and Miss One should count her blessings. She could search for years and perhaps never find anyone else quite like him.

Miss One has a mission in life. She desperately needs to express her unique individuality by leading the way for others to follow. She is confident, efficient, well-organized and certainly not afraid of hard work. She's original, perceptive and, like her partner Mr Six, also extremely creative in her own right. She leads a busy life but somehow she always manages to fit everything in. Mr Six likes to entertain and she is the perfect hostess. She is generous, forgiving, vital, energetic and occasionally a little eccentric which becomes more noticeable as the ageing process takes its inevitable toll. She is an attractive, sincere woman and provided she keeps a tight rein on that dominant personality of hers and tries not to lay down the law too often, all should be well in this relationship.

Their bedroom will almost certainly be dimly lit and romantic as Mr Six knows just how to create the right atmosphere. He is a dreamy, romantic person himself, given to long meaningful glances. Miss One is rather more down-to-earth although she can never resist praise or flattery especially when it comes from him. She is affectionate, demonstrative and certainly an exciting partner for any man lucky enough to have won her love. So shut the door, light the candles and let the handsome prince pay homage to his fair lady. And woe betide any dark knight who tries to steal her away; they will both chase him off because this relationship is likely to be for keeps and few can harm it.

Male Six:Female Two

This is not a particularly dynamic number combination as both partners are even, passive, receptive and introvert. It lacks the drive and ambition necessary for business success but on a personal level this relationship should work better than most. Mr Six and Miss Two tend to bring out the best in each other so their coexistence should be happy, harmonious and homely. The sum of Miss Two the homelover plus Mr Six the creator adds up to beauty, comfort and a balanced, promising outlook.

Mr Six is kindly, equable and conventional. He is very trusting and utterly trustworthy. He likes nothing better than peace and quiet, will go to great lengths to avoid arguments and simply loathes forceful, opinionated people. He possesses great charm, a magnetic personality and a fine brain. He is just, open-minded and capable of handling people with sympathy and understanding. He is reliable, honest and friendly. However he does have one burning, all-important need in life which is to be creative. He has excellent colour sense, a flair for art, literature and music and an eye for beauty. Whenever he feels restricted or unable to express his talents freely in a tangible way he soon becomes frustrated and downright miserable. He needs to paint, write or play just as much as he needs to breathe. In fact, any Six who has nothing to do and nowhere to go is a sorry sight indeed. He can be a particularly determined character and no one should ever stand in his way especially where his obsession is concerned.

Miss Two is rather shy and self-conscious. She hates making decisions and is likely to change her mind frequently. She needs encouragement and constant reassurance which she is sure to get from Mr Six and, at times, a strong shoulder to lean on which he is also bound to provide. She too is creative and superbly imaginative although rather more sensitive and thin-skinned than her partner. But behind that quiet exterior lies a humorous, sharp-witted conversationalist. She is tactful and concilitory, loves beauty, harmony and order and, surprisingly enough, can adapt to changing circumstances and events with apparent ease and charm. There really is more to this woman that at first meets the eye.

Miss Two prefers to follow rather than lead and needs to feel emotionally and financially secure at all times. She makes an excellent wife, a conscientious, caring mother and the ideal companion for Mr

Six. Domesticity suits her because home is where her heart is. On the negative side, she is moody, over-sensitive, prone to melancholy and imagines infidelities lurking behind every half-open wardrobe door. But Mr Six with his deep love and understanding is perhaps the one person who can help her overcome this difficulty, or at least get it into better perspective.

Mr Six is a romantic — the age of chivalry will never die while he's around. He is warmly affectionate, loyal, faithful and, secretly, just as anxious for fidelity as his partner. Miss Two is a gentle, sentimental woman and their lovemaking tends to be more spiritual than sensual and earthy. This couple seek emotional satisfaction and peace of mind; anything physical that they experience is merely an added bonus not a prerequisite.

Male Six:Female Three

Mr Six is one of those rare men who seem to get on well with almost any woman simply because he has such a warm, friendly air about him as well as being kind, thoughtful and a very good listener. Miss Three is certainly no exception to this rule and her personality is, in fact, much the same as his. When these two finally decide to name the day and set up house together their relationship, built on mutual trust, love, consideration and honesty, should withstand almost anything that life decides to throw at it. And once pledged they will almost certainly stay together.

Mr Six may be easy to get along with but he could never be called a 'ladies man'. He has many friends of both sexes and at a party he is usually surrounded by a whole crowd of people. He has the rare gift of intuitively understanding the needs and difficulties of others and somehow getting the best out of them. He is intelligent, imaginative and artistically talented. Not surprisingly his creativity is often reflected in his home. He is well-balanced, conventional and a real family man. Appearances count where Mr Six is concerned and if something doesn't look right he won't rest until it does.

One goal in his life is to be of service to others and to give help and support whenever it's called for. He certainly lives up to his ideals and is a charming man that many women would be proud to call their husband. He does have negative traits but none are particularly damaging.

He tends to be too helpful at times with the result that people become emotionally dependent upon him. And occasionally he will try to force his views upon others when his opinion has not been sought.

Miss Three is not only versatile but also clever, imaginative and amusing. She has a lively mind which is usually one step ahead of most others and a carefree attitude to life which can sometimes be her undoing. She has an inability to take anything too seriously and this is often mistaken for frivolity at the wrong moments. She is independent, shrewd, observant and full of original ideas. She is also creative and artistic, which is very much in tune with Mr Six.

She often does things on the spur of the moment and even apparent misfortunes for her have a way of turning out to be blessings in disguise. Fate rules her life, fortune smiles on her and luck is always at her side virtually every step of the way. Mr Six may find her a little lively but he will worship and adore her all the same. After all, how could he possibly resist such a happy, gifted lady as Miss Three?

Miss Three likes beautiful surroundings and their intimate, dimly-lit bedroom is probably her favourite room in the house. And it should be as they seem to spend a great deal of time there. Miss Three is warm, loving and spontaneous as well as exciting, unpredictable and full of fun. She is like a playful kitten and just as cuddly but Mr Six should never allow her to get bored because then she will show her claws. Stimulation and excitement is what this lady needs and she must find it in her relationship to feel truly fulfilled. Fortunately Mr Six should be man enough for the job. He is romantic, thoughtful and imaginative and if he can't create enough diversions for her then no one can.

Male Six:Female Four

Mr Six is a domesticated, peace-loving man. He never rocks the boat and certainly doesn't crave a life of drama or excitement. If his relationship is happy and incident-free this is ideal rather than merely satisfactory. His partner is a solid, practical, very down-to-earth woman. What she seeks is security and permanence in her personal life so if her liaison with Mr Six proves to be calm, organized and practically guaranteed nothing could suit her better. Perhaps to an outsider, this 6:4 combination seems stodgy and dull but for the couple involved it is perfect.

Mr Six is a family man. He is loving, compassionate and understanding. He takes his responsibilities seriously and is always ready to help out when someone he cares for runs into difficulties. He is intelligent, well-balanced, wholesome and conventional. He does his utmost to avoid forceful or opinionated people, will go to great lengths to side-step arguments and has the ability to see both sides of a problem. He's open-minded, self-controlled and reliable. He loves beauty, has an eye for colour and a very marked leaning towards the arts.

He has a passion for either painting, sculpture or music as well as a talent for writing. He is at his best when involved in some form of creative work and his home will always reflect this great love in one way or another.

Miss Four is a worker. She is energetic, industrious and very respectable. She is diplomatic, thoughtful, handles money wisely and, with care, is utterly trustworthy and reliable. She too is a homelover just like Mr Six; in fact she attaches great importance to family life. While she may not actively seek adventure fate seems to have a way of intervening in her life and she is likely to experience more than her fair share of unusual incidents and events during her time. She is sensitive and extremely self-disciplined, in fact there's nothing really sensational about her but Mr Six isn't a sensation seeker.

Their lovelife tends to be uneventful rather than a complete non-event. Mr Six is an affectionate, faithful man. His love is more romantic than sensual, he's sentimental, caring, considerate and gentle. And Miss Four is certainly no temptress. She has a down-to-earth approach to the intimate side of their relationship and while she can be tender and demonstrative she never goes over the top and loses complete control. It's moderation in all things for her.

Male Six:Female Five

A 6:5 combination is always something of an enigma because everything points to a disastrous relationship yet time and again these two manage to defy the odds and prove everyone wrong. When the temperamental, excitable Miss Five joins forces with a dove of peace she seems to undergo a very marked change in her personality. The calming influence of Mr Six enables her to think straight and once her thoughts are in order she will get a clearer view of life. While she may not have much to offer in material terms, she certainly makes up for it by being lively, adventurous and challenging. An ample reward for Mr Six.

Mr Six is equable, kind and well-balanced with a positive genius for home and family life and the rare gift of intuitively understanding the needs and difficulties of others and somehow getting the best out of them. He's just and kind with tremendous emotional and moral courage as well as being open-minded and self-controlled. He is loyal, faithful and utterly dependable. He enjoys entertaining family and friends, has an honest desire to make everyone happy and if there is one thing he cannot bear, or indeed tolerate, it's jealousy and discord. He avoids arguments, loathes forceful, opinionated people and likes nothing better than a quiet, peaceful, trouble-free existence.

Miss Five will certainly put the cat among the pigeons when she first comes on the scene because she's restless, jumpy and impatient. But once she has settled down to life with Mr Six, her better qualities should begin to show through. She is clever, many-sided, perceptive, selective, has impeccable taste, is fond of reading and remarkably well-informed. She has an elastic mind and does many things passably well. She is alert, original, creative and could be a highly successful artist or musician if only she would concentrate a little more. She does have many faults and to list them all would be an impossible task. She's thoughtless, impulsive, highly-strung, critical, sarcastic, unpredictable and self-indulgent. But all this will change with Mr Six. He handles people in such a way that they never seem to notice the influence he's exerting. He is one of the good guys and Miss Five should be putty in his expert hands.

In the bedroom they have other differences with which to come to terms. Mr Six is old-fashioned and leans to the romantic and ideal in all sexual matters. He is warmly affectionate, tender and sentimental so how is he going to deal with the insatiable Miss Five? Her number rules sexuality and animal instincts. She's adventurous, demonstrative and very demanding. This is one delicate problem he will have to handle with considerable tact if he wants to maintain the feeling of harmony he has built up between them.

Male Six:Female Six

Domestic bliss, beauty, comfort and complete happiness are usually found when two Sixes get together. They rarely have interests outside their home and family and simply live for each other in an atmosphere of mutual trust and adoration. Two Sixes will inevitably opt for marriage from the start not because they are conventional but simply because they are absolutely sure in their own minds that this is right. A trial period living together probably won't be necessary — they already know their relationship is going to work.

All Sixes possess moral and emotional courage. They are kindly and well-balanced with a talent for home and family life. They make conscientious parents, will often go to great lengths to avoid arguments and only really blow their tops when their sense of decency and honour is outraged. They are sympathetic, understanding people who are both trusting and trustworthy. They make excellent mediators and you can always rely on a Six to see both sides of a problem and to solve it impartially. Sixes are magnetic people with many good friends. They like to help others and are in a position to give support whenever it's needed.

Mr Six is a creative man who is usually at his happiest when doing something with his hands, while Miss Six is the motherly type. Sixes of both sexes love beautiful objects, rich colours and attractive surroundings. They often have the most unusual and interesting homes and always make their guests feel welcome and at ease.

Their lovemaking is warmly affectionate and considerate. They sometimes prefer to admire at a distance rather than come to grips with their passion. Love is something that should be treasured rather than taken as a purely physical union. This lucky couple should experience few problems in their relationship because they are completely in tune with one another.

Male Six:Female Seven

Mr Six and Miss Seven lack common ground for communication and this is why their relationship often breaks down. They're a perfect example of conflicting numbers (one even, one odd). When this happens physical attraction is rarely enough to keep a relationship off the rocks. There are marked differences of opinion, frequent clashes of personality and little basic understanding of each other's thoughts or motives.

Mr Six is artistic and spends so much time creating visual impressions that he hardly has a moment for Miss Seven's thoughts. She is very aloof and mysterious and always so absorbed in her wonderful fantasies that she never seems to notice what her partner is doing. Miss Seven is the one woman Mr Six really can't get on with. They would be well advised to nip their relationship quite ruthlessly in the bud before it blossoms into disaster. If they persist someone is likely to get badly hurt.

Male Six: Female Eight

'Potential' is undoubtedly the keyword here because the roles of each partner are clearly, if somewhat unconventionally, defined. Mr Six is happy to give support, offer the odd idea or two and provide a comfortable home. Miss Eight wants the best of both worlds — a career, a family and a well-run house. She's tough, aggressive and ambitious so why not let him stay at home? After all he is a homelover at heart.

Home has always been where Mr Six feels happiest and although at first Miss Eight's modern ideas seem rather alien to him he's perfectly prepared to give such an arrangement a try. He is sympathetic, generous and will always help out with boring and unpleasant jobs if someone he cares for cannot cope.

Miss Eight can cope perfectly well but domesticity doesn't suit her as much as it does him. Mr Six is kindly, equable and peacemaking with the rare gift of intuitively understanding the needs and difficulties of others and somehow getting the best out of them. He likes a quiet life and simply wants to make everyone around him as happy as possible. He does, however, suffer the odd tiny pangs of jealousy from time to time and will want to know exactly what Miss Eight is playing at if overtime becomes a permanent feature of her working life. Once married he prefers the company of his partner to that of anyone else so quite naturally he will want to share his evenings and weekends with her. Mr Six has marked ability in many fields of artistic ability. He is a fine musician, a talented artist, a dab hand at writing and a possible sculptor. He is at his best when involved in some kind of creative activity and by staying at home he will have ample time to put his talents to good use.

There is no doubt that Miss Eight is a go-getter. She is mercenary and doesn't care who knows it. Earning money appeals to her and it's something she does well. In fact her number stands for money, power and worldly involvement, so it is hardly surprising she feels the way she does. She is strong, practical and wise as well as being adaptable, hardworking and very self-disciplined. She has the ability to overcome setbacks and disappointments and will forge ahead with little support or encouragement to spur her on her way. She has an innate desire to succeed in life and will take advantage of every opportunity for advancement that happens to come her way. She is not afraid to speak her mind and can be hard, selfish and utterly ruthless when it comes to getting her own way.

Fortunately she has enough sense to leave her aggression at work because Mr Six cannot stand discord and argument. In private he seems to bring out the softer side of her personality with his gentle ways and warm affection. He is a romantic and although she tends to experience great extremes of emotion he very rarely fails to coax her into a tender, loving mood when they are alone.

Male Six:Female Nine

This relationship is always rather special because it combines beauty (six) with truth (nine). Mr Six and Miss Nine instinctively know how to give and take, on all levels of consciousness.

Six is the number of the peacemaker so naturally Mr Six tends to be kind, loving and considerate. He is understanding, compassionate and always responsive to the needs of others. He's sympathetic, well-balanced and very open-minded. Mr Six possesses moral and emotional courage, has the ability to get the best out of most people and because he can always see both sides in any argument he will always come up with an impartial solution to the problem in hand.

Mr Six is imaginative, idealistic, completely trusting and utterly trustworthy. He's a friendly person; easy to get along with; has a magnetic personality, charming manners and that old-fashioned courtesy so seldom seen these days. He's talented with a fine brain and a definite leaning to all matters artistic. He's also a family man who will do anything in his power to protect his loved ones and make them happy. He is a devoted husband, a conscientious father and the sort of friend who's always there when you need him. Mr Six is an honest, upright citizen.

Miss Nine is an incorrigible idealist. She needs more than anything to be of service to others and has an earnest desire to improve human life and make the world a better place in which to live. In a nutshell she's a 'do-gooder' but in the nicest possible way. Hope springs ever eternal in her breast and she has a 'never say die' attitude towards everything she attempts which sustains and uplifts her during times of trouble. She is determined, active and courageous but without the stubborn, tyrannical tendencies which often accompany these particular character traits. She has a clear, quick mind, great imagination and tremendous charm. She was born with exactly the same quota of artistic talent as Mr Six but in her case this is coupled with impulsiveness, passion and the odd unpredictable flash of inspiration. In fact she is almost certainly gifted with ESP perhaps in the form of clairvoyance or telepathy. Nine is the highest vibration of all and those born under its influence are strong-minded, powerful individuals. Miss Nine is no exception; she is a woman of high mental and spiritual achievement.

The intimate side of this relationship should have an ethereal air about it; a union of minds rather than a purely physical demonstration of this couple's undoubted love for each other. Mr Six is the romantic type — tender, considerate and sentimental. Miss Nine is also a romantic but she does come down to earth a little more often. When the mood takes her she can be a fiery, passionate, impulsive creature and Mr Six could find her a handful at such times.

Male Seven:Female One

The couple here need to express themselves in different ways even though both their numbers are odd and such a combination, when it happens, usually indicates grounds for a harmonious coexistence. They should bring out the best rather than the worst in each other but it doesn't always happen like that as we shall discover when we look more closely at each character.

Miss One is a 'doer', Mr Seven a 'thinker' and he, in particular, needs to spend a great deal of time on his own in order to reflect on and regiment his thoughts. However, if they are both prepared to make allowances for each other's needs then their partnership should come to fruition.

Mr Seven is a loner. His needs are few and simple. He cares little for money and marginally less for physical comforts. His is the magic number and by definition he is magical, mysterious and infuriatingly secretive. He has a powerful mind and the ability to penetrate the unknown, combining the practical with the theoretical and the accepted with the unacceptable.

He is highly imaginative, studious, creative and irresistibly attracted towards the occult and mysticism. He has unconventional ideas about religion, strange predictive dreams, the gifts of intuition and clairvoyance, and a peculiar quieting magnetism all of his own which greatly influences those around him. He can somehow manage to curb Miss One's tendency to act without thought and generates ideas which she is well-equipped to promote in her work. He loves to travel but often in a spartan fashion. He may not be down to earth, practical or reliable but one thing is certain, he's a very interesting man once you break the ice and get to know him. His words are pure wisdom and his knowledge unique.

Miss One is the archetypal career woman although she echoes Mr Seven's personality in many ways. She has a pioneering spirit running in her veins but unlike Mr Seven, it's on a more material plane. She sets little store by friendship or co-operation — all Ones are inclined to put themselves first and she's no exception. Mr Seven may be selfish about his 'thinking time' but she can be just as bad, if not worse, when she wants to get something done.

Miss One is independent, single-minded and purposeful. She has a deep sense of responsibility, a tremendous desire to succeed and a well-organized mind to ensure that she does. Like Mr Seven, travel appeals to her because it represents an opportunity for new experiences. However, it will have to be first class.

She is intelligent, logical, drawn to the new and unusual and very well equipped to argue far into the night over the finer points of her partner's philosophies. Like everyone else she does have her bad points which manifest themselves in the form of obstinacy, aggressiveness and an unreasonable dislike of restraint but these unfortunate negative traits are outweighed by her charm, her sincerity and her generous, forgiving nature.

When Mr Seven eventually takes time off and gives a thought to the intimate side of his relationship or, for that matter, Miss One isn't feeling too exhausted after a hard day's work, then these two are a pair of strangely well-matched bedfellows. Mr Seven is passionate, emotional and very imaginative. He makes love with his mind as well as his body and with Miss One he usually gains complete satisfaction on both planes; the physical and the spiritual. Miss One is vital and energetic about everything she attempts. She is adventurous, demonstrative and always prepared to initiate matters whenever necessary.

Male Seven:Female Two

Mr Seven and Miss Two are a very spiritual pair and seem in complete agreement most of the time. This number combination is so peaceful and harmonious that a little injection of friction can be a good thing to ensure that they don't become too smug and self-satisfied.

Mr Seven's mission in life is to develop his mind in order to gain wisdom and understanding. And he often does this to the exclusion of all else. If he hasn't actually got his nose buried in a book, he will be so deeply engrossed in thought that he won't even notice someone enter the room. He is studious, intellectual and very philosophical in his attitude to life.

Mr Seven is reserved, dignified, aloof and artistic. He prefers, on occasion, to be left alone to reflect and meditate, and cares little for money and physical comfort. He is not particularly ambitious or career-minded but, once married, he soon pulls his socks up to provide a comfortable home for his loved ones. He is a mysterious, private sort of man much given to secrecy and strongly attracted to magic and the occult. He seems unable to accept the more traditional explanations concerning the nature and meaning of existence and uses all his energy and intellect to explore the world about him.

Miss Two finds him attractive, fascinating and awe-inspiring all at once. She's rather shy, terribly self-conscious, infuriatingly hesitant and very indecisive. She is quiet, tactful, conciliatory, conscientious and modest. She loves peace and harmony on one hand and loathes discord and anger on the other. She is a born follower, receptive to new ideas, deeply intuitive and also rather clairvoyant and mystical herself at times.

Now we come to the friction which is needed to put some spice into this relationship and Miss Two is the one with that particular ingredient. She's possessive, jealous and moody. She sulks, pouts, cries and mopes when things don't go right. These negative character traits should provide more than enough abrasion to keep complacency at bay.

In private their moments of intimacy should be a source of great joy to them both. Mr Seven will always lead the way in lovemaking and Miss Two will usually respond eagerly and willingly to his advances. He is understanding, emotional and passionate, experiencing his pleasures on two different planes at once while she is gentle, imaginative, romantic and even still a little on the shy side. The overall, long-term outlook is very promising for both.

Male Seven:Female Three

Although we're dealing with two odd numbers, Mr Seven and Miss Three should always allow each other sufficient room to move within this relationship. Mr Seven's need to spend some time on his own is vital. It is crucial for his 'inner development' and should never be denied him by Miss Three. She too has her faults and they manifest themselves in her inability to take few things seriously, her wastefulness and her pride. The first is the most important for her to curb, especially when Mr Seven is around, because he's not a frivolous man.

Mr Seven is always a secretive, mysterious person because he was born under the vibration of the magic number. He is studious, intellectual and highly imaginative. He has a powerful mind which he uses to search for the truth behind his day to day existence. He's a philosopher, a dreamer, a mystic and a student of life. He is not particularly career-minded or indeed interested in money or personal comfort. He is reserved, dignified and artistic although pleasant, good-natured and understanding too. In fact he's an interesting, knowledgeable man — one who is well worth getting to know better.

Three is the number of enlightenment and Miss Three is brilliant, imaginative and extremely versatile. She is charming, lively, creative and highly talented. She is ambitious and once married will probably decide to continue pursuing her career. This is where her adaptability will come in very handy. Here is a woman who can successfully run her life on two different wavelengths without problems. She will switch with ease from capable business woman one moment to devoted wife and mother the next. She has a fine brain and can easily concentrate on more than one thing at a time. She is able to think clearly at great speed, will amost always emerge the victor in a battle of wits and takes a secret delight in running mental rings around those with slower minds. However, it's doubtful whether Mr Seven will let her get away with this for very long. He is one of the few men she won't be able to outsmart all the time.

When it comes to a physical display of their emotions this couple are remarkably well-matched and shouldn't experience any insuperable problems in this area. Mr Seven is an exciting, unpredictable lover, passionate, emotional and inventive. Miss Three is warm and impulsive. She is neither jealous nor possessive but does need to be amused. At the first hint of boredom she is off like a startled horse but she won't bolt from this relationship because Mr Seven is far too mysterious and intriguing for that to happen.

Male Seven:Female Four

This pair could rarely be described as perfect or ideal. What is missing in this relationship is spiritual rapport and while these two are able to communicate well on Miss Four's practical, down-to-earth level it takes a Herculean effort for her to follow some of Mr Seven's philosophies.

Mr Seven, born under the magic number and heavily influenced by its mystical vibrations, needs to develop his mind to gain wisdom and understanding. He thinks, he meditates, he studies and he constantly searches for the truth. He wants to solve the riddles of life and will use his knowledge unselfishly to guide other true seekers onto the right path. Miss Four finds this all too difficult but she will eventually fall under the spell of his special magnetism.

He is artistic, dreamy, imaginative and a dreadful, absent-minded muddler. However, the highly-organized Miss Four will soon have all his books and papers catalogued and indexed for him. Mr Seven is a pleasant, if rather reserved man. He is good-natured, hates arguments and will be only too willing for her to become his administrator, housekeeper and much-loved wife. She is calm, steady, and reliable and while she may never share his fantasy world or accompany him on his mental journeys, she'll provide a strong anchor to keep him firmly in touch with the everyday world.

Miss Four is hard-working and industrious. She is good at handling money, stolid, self-disciplined and, above all, unflappable. She's domesticated, home-loving and very good company. She has an inventive if somewhat mechanical mind, an infectious laugh and a whole host of amusing stories to recount. And Mr Seven could do with seeing the funny side of life. Deep down she is a sensitive woman and when her feelings have been trampled on she tends to get gloomy and depressed.

Mr Seven and Miss Four are an unlikely pair of bedfellows. Nevertheless they often seem to be content with the physical side of their relationship. And, even when they're not, neither of them complains very loudly about it. Mr Seven is emotional, passionate, imaginative and understanding. There is nothing forceful or pushy about him and when she's not in the mood, then he is quite prepared to wait. Miss Four is sentimental, faithful and considerate. Her needs may not be as great as his but if Tuesdays, Thursdays and every alternate Saturday suits him then that will fit in nicely with her routine too — she always has to have one. Neither of them are particularly jealous or possessive and while they may not experience as many 'highs' as some other couples, their 'lows' are also few and far between.

Male Seven:Female Five

This combination has the potential for disaster — it's a mixture of fire and water. Mr Seven needs time to think, he needs peace and tranquillity but Miss Five is the person least likely to help him create a calm, unruffled atmosphere.

One of the few things this couple could share is their mutual love of travel but even here they probably won't see eye to eye. Mr Seven likes to travel light, roughing it if necessary and preferring to get off the beaten track as soon as possible. But Miss Five wants to do everything in style; staying at five-star hotels in smart, trendy resorts where even the sunshine is guaranteed.

A redeeming factor is their lovemaking which can be sensational to say the least because she is ruled by five, the number of pure sexuality, and he comes under the influence of the magic number of seven which makes him highly imaginative. As a passing affair their union should be memorable, if somewhat stormy, but once they decide to enter into a permanent relationship it can usually lead only one way — to disappointment, bitter regrets and separation.

Male Seven:Female Six

Looking back to the 6:7 combination where the numerological male/female roles are reversed (page 111) we see a relationship fraught with problems. But with the numbers the other way round the relationship is entirely different. Instead of fighting one another, Mr Seven and Miss Six pull together in complete unison.

Mr Seven is a brilliant, unusual character. He is studious, creative and highly imaginative although his creativity usually takes the form of thoughts and ideas rather than Miss Six's more tangible efforts. He is intellectual, independent and original with an off-beat, philosophical outlook.

He finds traditional views and explanations hard to accept and is always striving to uncover new truths in unconventional ways. Money and physical comfort mean little to him but he's a considerate, understanding man and once deeply committed he will make every effort to provide a beautiful, comfortable home for his loved ones. There is always something very strange, magnetic and magical about Mr Seven which attracts people to him.

He is dignified, reserved, sometimes rather aloof but always good-natured, pleasant and ready to put his knowledge and wisdom at the disposal of others if he feels it will benefit them. What he needs most of all is peace and quiet and Miss Six, with the white dove as her symbol, will ensure that his life is free from troubles.

Miss Six is intelligent, well-balanced and motherly. She has a talent for home and family life and because she's sympathetic, caring and generous with her time she soon finds even complete strangers telling her their problems as if she had known them for years. She is open-minded, self-controlled and makes an excellent mediator. She is adept at handling people; has the rare gift of intuitively understanding their needs and difficulties; and somehow manages to get the best from them. She also has a special talent in the field of art.

Miss Six leans to the romantic and ideal in her affections — her love is more spiritual than sensual. Her feathers could get a little ruffled with Mr Seven as her lover because still waters run deep and beneath the surface he's a passionate, emotional man. He is imaginative, demonstrative and may be rather more red-blooded than she originally bargained for. However, she is good at solving problems, and he is patient, so any physical problems in this relationship will almost certainly be resolved in time.

Male Seven:Female Seven

A combination of Sevens is sheer perfection. Arguments between them are rare because they are completely in tune with each other. However, Sevens tend to create a dream world of their own, a world entirely peopled with concepts and ideas totally divorced from reality. They need to exercise care and constraint to ensure that they don't lose their realism and should make every effort to develop a more materialistic outlook.

Sevens are all very much alike, be they male or female, young or old, so when describing Mr Seven's character and make-up we are also talking about his partner, Miss Seven. He is a brilliant, unusual individual who likes to be left in peace. He's scholarly, philosophical, intellectual and has the ability to penetrate the unknown combining the practical and theoretical, the accepted and the unconventional. He is unwilling to take accepted views at face value and uses his intellect to search for new truths. He's well-informed and has a great love of travel. However, on the negative side, he can be aloof, confusing, lazy, pessimistic and sarcastic.

When he and Miss Seven get together nothing could be better because they think, act and feel in unison. This can be a truly harmonious, rewarding relationship and one which would be difficult to equal in terms of emotional and spiritual satisfaction.

Intimacy, when two Sevens are involved, is a celebration of mind, body and spirit which they experience on all three levels of consciousness. They are both emotional, passionate individuals without any possessive hang-ups or even the slightest suspicion of jealousy between them. They are demonstrative, creative, imaginative and, of course, unconventional. Their vibrations are exactly the same; the tunes they play together on their own special wavelength have a strange, ethereal quality about them and they are, above all, blissfully happy in each other's company.

Male Seven:Female Eight

In private life this 7:8 combination can be excellent although both people have different types of character and personality. In fact they are a fine example of opposites who not only attract but also manage to achieve a working balance. The outlook for this relationship is promising provided Miss Eight doesn't become too bossy (which is her main and perhaps worst fault) and that Mr Seven pays sufficient court to the gentle art of conversation.

Mr Seven, ruled by the magic number which governs solitude and knowledge, is a secretive, enigmatic man. He is mysterious, creative, artistic and intellectual. In a negative frame of mind he will often appear aloof, confusing and sarcastic but normally he is extremely good-natured. He has a powerful, penetrating mind and needs to spend a great deal of time on his own just contemplating, meditating and thinking in order to further his 'inner growth'. He is highly imaginative and, unless he is careful, his advanced intuitive powers could carry him far beyond the bounds of reality. He loves to travel; is an avid reader, and is keenly interested in the affairs and cultures of far-off lands and with a wide, universal knowledge of the world around him.

Miss Eight is an ambitious, career-minded materialist so what on earth is she doing with a mysterious truth seeker like Mr Seven? She is wise and imaginative too but also tough, strong and practical. She craves success, recognition and monetary rewards. All he wants is peace, insight and the answers to some pretty tough questions. When seen at her best she is charming, dignified, tireless and tenacious but when the moon is in the wrong quarter she can be hard, selfish and unscrupulous. Her number is one of great reversals and throughout her life she suffers great extremes of emotion. It's a problem she has to live with and Mr Seven is likely to be able to cope with it.

Lovemaking is the greatest stumbling block for them and Miss Eight is probably the main cause of their problems. She is either in the mood for love or she's not; there is never a happy medium. To make matters worse she is incurably jealous. Their bedroom is rather like a minefield and poor Mr Seven has to tread with great care each night as he makes his way hesitantly towards their bed. He never knows what he will encounter on the way or indeed what to expect when he gets there. He is a passionate lover made all the more exciting by his imagination, originality and unconventionality but he can't stand his patience being tried for too long!

Male Seven:Female Nine

Peace, harmony and understanding are all qualities to be found in abundance within a 7:9 relationship. Mr Seven and Miss Nine are living proof of the old adage that great minds think alike; they both have fine brains and seldom appear to disagree. But as with all spiritual combinations the great danger is that they will become too spiritual and lose touch with the everyday world of reality. If they remember to come down to earth from time to time, their relationship should continue and increase in strength as it goes along.

Mr Seven is magical, mysterious and secretive. He needs to spend time alone in order to recharge his brain cells through thought, meditation and reflection. He's an unusual, intellectual character; sometimes rather aloof but generally good-natured, pleasant and kind. He is creative, artistic and philosophical. His number governs occult mysteries, clairvoyance, magical operations and knowledge so his mission here on earth is to study, learn, search for truth and attempt to find the answers to life's riddles. His mind must be developed to the full in order to gain wisdom and knowledge and he follows his chosen path with true dedication and an earnest desire to fulfil his role. He is independent, original and very spartan. He loves to travel and has unconventional ideas about most things including religion. He hates arguments and is always ready to draw upon his store of learning in a sincere desire to help others who have sought his advice. He is a wise old bird just like his symbol, the owl, and the perfect partner for an unorthodox visionary such as Miss Nine.

Miss Nine is a woman of high mental and spiritual achievement. She is large-minded, idealistic and very determined in all she attempts. She relies upon her instincts and is susceptible to unpredictable flashes of inspiration. She is honest, trusting, resourceful and enterprising. She needs to be of service to others and is at her best when involved in some humanitarian scheme. She is loyal, unselfish, willing and also eccentric at times. Impulsiveness is her biggest fault — if she would take the time to think a little more often before she speaks or acts she could avoid many problems. But perhaps Mr Seven will be able to calm her down at such times. Seven is the magical number, Nine is mystical and it all adds up to a very special relationship indeed.

There are no nasty demons like jealousy, possessiveness or physical indifference overshadowing their lovemaking. Moments of intimacy should be both sensual and ethereal. Mr Seven is an emotional passionate man while Miss Nine is romantic, enthusiastic and impulsive. This relationship certainly embodies something very rare.

Male Eight:Female One

This relationship is made up of some powerful ingredients including courage, determination and ambition. Both individuals will need to keep a tight rein on their forceful natures. A combination like this will either be a resounding success or an unmitigated disaster; there are no shades of grey as far as these proud, aggressive people are concerned.

Mr Eight is the stereotype business man. He has an innate desire to succeed in life and is well equipped to take advantage of every opportunity for advancement. His sights are set on money and social position and he will work day and night if necessary to accomplish his ends. He is strong, adaptable, self-disciplined and practical and, when sufficiently motivated, hard, selfish and utterly ruthless. Most of his knowledge has been gained the hard way through personal experience. He is dignified, charming and tough. Eight is a difficult vibration to live under as it's a number of great reversals and the failures of people influenced by it can be as spectacular as their successes. From a negative viewpoint, Mr Eight is domineering, unscrupulous and argumentative but when seen at his best he is extremely cool, poised and memorable.

Miss One is the stereotype career woman. She has great purpose and a tremendous drive. On the surface she is charming, attractive, affectionate and sincere but anyone who crosses her will soon discover quite a different side to her nature when she becomes impatient, obstinate, intolerant and downright aggressive. She is positive, active and daring with excellent powers of concentration and a retentive memory. She has a superb, creative imagination, the curiosity of a cat and the capacity to adjust bravely to even the most depressing circumstances. Miss One is efficient in an emergency, tackles her responsibilities unflinchingly and has a marked talent for leadership. She has strong views and opinions, an intense dislike of restraint and an overwhelming desire to excel at whatever she does. Mr Eight will need to handle her with care because this woman fights. In fact both of them will need to exercise great tact and discretion within this relationship if they want it to survive.

Mr Eight makes a loyal, devoted lover but he does need constant reassurance of his partner's fidelity because he suffers the sharp pangs of jealousy at the slightest opportunity. His emotions are always in a turmoil and he swings from being gentle, caring and demonstrative one moment to brusque and detached the next. He is like a see-saw and Miss One will need to gauge which way the wind is blowing very carefully before she makes one of her spontaneous, amorous advances or she could find herself facing rejection — something she's not prepared to take too often. She is affectionate, adventurous and impatient. Fortunately she is also generous and reasonably forgiving and these qualities will frequently be put to the test when she shares a bed with Mr Eight. Their lovemaking can be exceptional but it can also become non-existent and should this breakdown in physical communications continue for long periods at a time it could eventually signpost the way to separation. Mr Eight is usually the one at fault here and should try harder if he wants to keep Miss One to himself. She is full of initiative and this could take her into the arms of someone else if he doesn't mend his ways.

Male Eight: Female Two

Mr Eight and Miss Two are a couple who seem to have got the formula right and they manage to live together in peace and harmony because they don't tread on each other's toes; or at least not often enough to do any permanent damage. They are both honest, industrious, reliable and their frankness with each other enables them to gauge exactly where they stand at all times. Mr Eight can be a bit naughty when he allows his dynamic personality to eclipse that of Miss Two especially in company, but as she never seems to have the slightest inclination to take the limelight for herself this does no real harm. In fact Miss Two prefers to take a back seat even though her partner can be a dangerously aggressive driver, particularly when he's in a hurry to get where he's going.

Strong, tough and practical is a fair description of Mr Eight. His is the number of worldly involvement, earthly triumph and material success (or failure). Mammon is his god; he saw the light from his cradle and has followed money ever since. He's a materialist through and through and has very few values in life other than monetary ones. He needs to succeed and, what's more, to be seen to have done so. He wants social recognition, status symbols and a decorative woman on his arm.

Mr Eight is wise, imaginative and intense with vast reserves of creative energy which he can bring into play at any time of the day or night. He's hard-working, well organized, self-assured, self-controlled and self-motivated. He is going to make it to the top come hell or high water and he's hard, selfish and sufficiently ruthless to do it. Miss Two could have a tough time with her charming, dignified partner because he sometimes finds it difficult to express his affection.

Miss Two needs to be directed almost as much as she needs a strong man to rely on. Two is a neutral number and those influenced by it can be good or evil by a combination of factors. Miss Two is easily influenced and indecisive; she frequently changes her mind but Mr Eight will step in here. She is generally shy and self-conscious although this can be deceptive because once she comes out of her shell she is surprisingly humorous, sharp-witted and a fascinating conversationalist.

She is tactful and conciliatory, creative, imagination and deeply intuitive. She does, however, have one great problem and that is her changing moods. She is over-sensitive, easily hurt, possessive and jealous. She will need to harden up to cope with Mr Eight as, beneath that poised, unruffled exterior, he too suffers similar problems.

It is very difficult to say how their moments of intimacy will turn out because so much depends upon the mood they are in at the time. On a good night, when her moon is in the right quarter and he's done well at work all should be sweetness and light.

Male Eight:Female Three

When Mr Eight and Miss Three join forces their relationship is often middle of the road. Their numbers are conflicting (one even, one odd) which indicates the occasional clash of personality as well as a fair sprinkling of misunderstanding but nothing a little give and take won't put to right.

Mr Eight's number comes from the 'business' trio so it is no great surprise when we discover that he's a budding tycoon. Miss Three falls within the 'expression' category which means she is gifted, creative and artistic. No immediate problems seem apparent and this combination should be harmonious, compatible and rewarding at all levels. And while they could never be described as the perfect couple the scales are tipped in their favour.

Mr Eight makes no secret of the fact that he is ambitious. His innate desire is to be a success and he works tirelessly and relentlessly to accomplish his objectives. He craves power and authority and never misses a trick, as far as advancement is concerned, in his long, hard fight to the top of the heap. He is strong, tough and practical. Most of his vast store of knowledge has been gained from first-hand experience; he is adaptable, responsible and reliable. He uses his resources intelligently and can be hard and ruthless when the need arises. He is self-motivated, self-disciplined and self-propelled. He does tend to be rather more aggressive at times than circumstances warrant and regards a certain amount of quarrelling as perfectly normal. He is a hard-headed, hard-hitting sometimes hard-hearted go-getter and Miss Three will need to stick up for herself is she doesn't want him to ride rough-shod over her.

However, there is nothing shy or retiring about Miss Three. She is witty, charming and full of life. She's brilliant, imaginative and versatile, expressing herself boldly and with style. She is observant, shrewd and talented, full of original ideas and inventive plans to execute them. She has a keen brain, thinks at alarmingly high speeds and can usually run mental rings around those with slower minds. She is generally one step ahead of everyone else, including Mr Eight at times.

Miss Three is inclined to call a spade a spade even when tact and discretion would have been preferable. Her direct manner of speech can often unwittingly give offence but where Mr Eight is concerned it's probably her best line of both defence and attack. She is warm, charming and impulsively generous. Her main fault is her inability to take anything seriously, with frivolity and wastefulness coming in close seconds. She will certainly need all her wits about her in this relationship and her lucky streak could also be a blessing too.

Mr Eight and Miss Three may not exactly be star-struck lovers but they are a well-matched pair each with their own particular strengths and weaknesses. Mr Eight's Achilles' heel is his jealousy. When his partner really wants to wind him up she has only to hint that someone else finds her attractive, then stand well back and wait for the inevitable fireworks to ensue. He is subject to great extremes of emotion and as a lover his moods are unpredictable and extremely changeable. He can be ardent and demanding one moment and cool and detached the next. Fortunately Miss Three doesn't have any hang-ups where lovemaking is concerned. She is warm, impulsive, easy-going and adaptable. She is not particularly jealous or possessive but quite capable of ending a relationship if driven to it and moody Mr Eight had better believe it.

Male Eight:Female Four

The combination of Mr Eight and Miss Four is really rather like a pair of scales. Without any undue effort or great strain they manage to achieve perfect balance within their relationship simply because they look at life, and all its attendant problems, from the same viewpoint.

Mr Eight sees everything on a large scale while Miss Four has an eye for detail. Between them they can usually manage to nip most problems swiftly in the bud long before they have time to blossom and cause any great damage to their relationship. Nothing very much ever seems to slip through their protective net and the result is a happy, well-balanced partnership built on such solid foundations as trust, consideration and wisdom.

Eight is the number of money, power and worldly involvement; of material success (or failure), and Mr Eight is strong, tough, practical and overtly ambitious. He wants to do exceptionally well for himself and to earn financial rewards as well as social status. He is intelligent, knowledgeable and imaginative with tremendous creative energy and the ability to forge ahead without encouragement or support. He is responsible, truthful, reliable, adaptable and able to overcome obstacles without losing heart or indeed sight of his ultimate goal. He is cool, calm, collected and utterly charming but when his hopes are set exceptionally high (even by his standards) then he will take advantage of any and every opportunity for advancement. When he's in a particularly determined frame of mind he can be hard, selfish, aggressive and totally without scruples. He works hard, plays hard and only the very best is good enough for him. The materialistic Mr Eight will get to the top even if the effort nearly kills him because that is the way he is made and second best just won't do.

Miss Four is a replica of her partner. She too is solid, practical, hard-working and energetic although perhaps a little more down to earth than he is. She's calm, efficient and extremely well-organized. She is patient, persevering and never tempted to give up even when the going gets difficult. Hers is the number of foundation and endurance. Miss Four is a builder and constructs her life one brick at a time until she has erected her own monument to achievement through sheer hard work. She is stimulating company; a good conversationalist; has a fine inventive brain and the most infectious of laughs. Above all, she's conventional, respectable, tenacious and utterly trustworthy. This homeloving, thoughtful woman makes the ideal partner for Mr Eight and together they should go far.

Mr Eight usually finds intimate situations rather difficult to handle because he always experiences problems in expressing his affections. Coupled with this, he is also subject to great extremes of emotion which means that even when he happens to be in a loving mood, he doesn't always approach the matter well. Jealousy and possessiveness are two more of his faults so all in all he's an unpredictable man to share a bed with. Deep down he may well be loyal and devoted, unfortunately it's on the surface that his blemishes appear. However, Miss Four is far too sensible to let his hang-ups spoil an otherwise perfect relationship. She is sentimental, faithful and considerate with no particular sexual problems of her own and, given time, she is the woman who can straighten him out. She never allows anything to stand in her way, least of all a moody, peevish Mr Eight clad only in pyjamas to cover his dignity. Love will find a way for this couple but it might take them quite a time to discover the right path.

Male Eight:Female Five

Mr Eight and Miss Five are an odd amalgam of talents and temperaments. They are two hyper-dynamic people and the combination can be a real winner while it lasts. Unfortunately durability isn't one of the keywords here and a relationship like this does tend to burn itself out fairly quickly if someone doesn't apply the brakes in time. This couple do everything at high speed; they crave new experiences, adventure, excitement and, in Miss Five's case, danger too. They cut corners, take the most appalling risks and, when matters have finally got out of hand, the crash comes and their relationship lies in ruins at their feet. The occasional thrills and spills are all very well, but not twenty-four hours a day, seven days a week; moderation is what is needed and without it they are heading for very serious trouble.

Mr Eight has a mission in life; he needs to be materially successful and to have authority. He is ambitious, strong and aggressive, working tirelessly day and night to accomplish his objectives. He is tough, practical, wise, imaginative and full to the brim with creative energy. Obstacles, set-backs and disappointments seldom get him down for long and he is soon to be seen forging ahead again without help or support from anyone. Unfortunately, he does have a very blinkered outlook and all his values are purely material ones. He makes no secret of his desires, takes advantage of any and every opportunity for advancement that comes his way and can be hard, selfish and utterly ruthless. He is tough, with a hide like a rhinoceros; he is dignified, self-controlled, charming and probably a complete emotional mess.

Mr Eight has a deep, intense nature and is subject to great extremes of feeling. Eight is the number of reversals; of resounding successes or spectacular failures; of highs and lows; of enthusiasm or disinterest. There is never a happy medium and Mr Eight's fortunes could go either way, both at work and in his private affairs.

Miss Five isn't rich, and is certainly not successful because she never sticks to anything for more than five minutes at a time but she can still be useful to Mr Eight simply because she has style and there's nothing he likes better than to be seen with an elegant, attractive woman at his side. But whether he can keep this restless, impatient creature there for long is another matter because she is extremely astute and seldom wastes her time on unrealistic schemes, enterprises or people. She is quick in thought, impulsive in her actions, unpredictable, inconsiderate and self-indulgent. While Mr Eight is amusing she will stay around but once his mood begins to change she'll be off without a moment's hesitation. Miss Five is clever, original and creative; quick-tempered and physically very demonstrative and demanding. She is mercurial and, like quicksilver, will soon run through his fingers and be lost if he doesn't treat her with care.

In the bedroom their encounters will certainly be close but of an entirely different kind to most others. Mr Eight generally has difficulty in expressing his affections at the best of times and to make matters worse has extremely changeable attitudes. One minute he can be cool and detached while the next he is gentle and sympathetic. He's also jealous and this brings other problems to their relationship. With his moods and false accusations he can be a real passion-killer when he feels like it. Five is the number of sexuality and Miss Five is heavily influenced by its vibrations. She is sensual, adventurous, tireless and never easily satisfied. Mr Eight may have his moments but they will need to become more frequent to keep up with her needs. This relationship has potential but its requires a great deal of consistent hard work plus a few minor miracles to keep it in a state of good repair for any length of time.

Male Eight:Female Six

Mr Eight and Miss Six make an excellent team because she is always prepared to give and he is always ready to accept. Mr Eight is the breadwinner, a role he plays to perfection, while his peaceloving partner with her flair for homemaking plays her part capably and with style. Within this relationship the role of each partner is clearly defined and as they don't overlap in any way they seldom step on each other's toes. The formula for their success is a simple but faultless one; he provides the wherewithall and she the trimmings.

Mr Eight is a man of the world — strong, tough, practical and ambitious. He works hard and untiringly because his sights are set high on great wealth and social status. He's virtually unstoppable, never allows anyone or anything to stand in his way and is quite prepared to be hard, selfish, ruthless and unscrupulous in the pursuit of his ends. He is the original self-made man. He is adaptable, responsible, self-disciplined, imaginative and marshalls his resources with intelligence and foresight. If anyone deserves to succeed it must be him.

Eight is a difficult vibration to live under at the best of times because it's a number of extremes so if Mr Eight doesn't manage to make the grade one thing is certain, he will fail in the most spectacular, head-line manner imaginable. There's nothing mediocre about him, least of all his mistakes. He is larger than life and twice as determined.

Miss Six is equable, well-balanced and sympathetic. She has a magnetic personality and people are attracted, and often captivated, by her sunny disposition and rather old-fashioned charm; especially Mr Eight. She is a talented lady with artistic leanings. She is wholesome, conventional and usually at her best when involved in some kind of creative activity. Miss Six is intelligent, open-minded and self-controlled. She's not particularly interested in money so long as things are running smoothly (she'll leave their finances to him), although she doesn't like waste and is usually very economical. She is honest, domesticated, a born wife and a considerate mother. Miss Six has both moral and emotional courage, a way of handling people, and intuitively understanding their needs and difficulties. Mr Eight will need a great deal of understanding and careful handling because his emotions are usually in a muddle but she will soon find a way to bring out his better qualities and he will be a nicer person for her efforts. He is in safe, loving hands and only good can come from their relationship.

Mr Eight is not the easiest of men to get along with at an intimate level because he experiences difficulty in expressing his feelings and is subject to great extremes of emotion. He's also jealous and incurably possessive. However, with Miss Six as his partner his problems should soon come to an end. She is a motherly woman rather than a sensual tigress and once she had cuddled up to him, reassured him of her fidelity and has told him a few bedtime stories he will be putty in her hands. Deep down he can be such an old softie; it just takes the right woman to discover the best way to his heart. Not surprisingly Miss Six is a first class cook bordering on the cordon bleu so let's hope she doesn't fatten him up too much with her culinary delights while she's trying to find the right way.

Male Eight:Female Seven

Take the materialistic Mr Eight and put him with the mysterious Miss Seven and the result could be murder, mayhem or sheer magic. One thing is certain, something very positive will come from their relationship but whether the result is good or bad will be entirely up to them. Miss Seven has a visionary quality about her which can be vital when Mr Eight is making plans, she is also rather inclined to be philosophical and spiritual which will add depth to his otherwise mercenary outlook. But how long can she put up with his quarrelsome nature, his bossiness, his peculiar changeable moods and his insane jealousy? The answer to that question is — almost indefinitely. She will either ignore him completely or withdraw into silence and only come out when the storm has passed. If she continues to adopt this attitude then these two could go on forever. Once has has discovered that she is not prepared to scrap and argue with him, he will soon calm down and settle into a peaceful, harmonious way of life with the pleasant, good-natured Miss Seven at his side taking full responsibility for his 'inner' development.

Mr Eight is hard-working, hard-headed and hard-hitting. He's a big businessman, an entrepreneur, a tycoon, a mogul; Mammon is his god. He is strong, tough and practical although quite prepared to go one step further in his quest for fame and fortune when circumstances dictate. Then he becomes aggressive, domineering, utterly ruthless and totally without scruples. He will forge ahead without support or encouragement, taking obstacles and set-backs in his stride; he uses his resources with intelligence and foresight and takes every opportunity for advancement that comes his way. He is self-disciplined, responsible, adaptable and creative. Most of his knowledge comes from experience rather than textbooks, and he has remarkably sound judgement and undoubted powers of leadership.

Eight is a number of extremes and people born under this vibration have no happy medium. In other words, they never take the middle path through life; it's a case of all or nothing as far as they are concerned. Mr Eight is not an easy man to weigh up but once Miss Seven has got to work on him. then he will find it easier to understand, and indeed control, his moods.

Miss Seven is indepedent, original and very creative. She is an interesting, intellectual woman and not Mr Eight's usual 'flashy' type at all. She has a questioning mind and highly advanced intuitive and imaginative powers. She is reserved, dignified and artistic. Her needs are modest and, unlike him, she cares little for money or physical comfort. Miss Seven is studious, quiet, self-contained and secretive, has peculiar ideas about religion, the gift of clairvoyance and a great leaning to the occult. She is wise and knowledgeable on a great many subjects, loves to travel, wants to find the answers to life's riddles and needs to spend at least some time on her own each day to think, meditate and reflect.

Mr Eight finds her need to be alone coupled with her secrecy intensely irritating because he always wants to know what she's up to and what she's thinking about. And when she doesn't choose to explain her actions he flies into a tantrum of magnificent rage. However, unpleasantness disturbs her and she will usually insist that the problem is discussed immediately in a sincere desire to clear the air.

This couple could experience many storms, and even the occasional hurricane during their moments of intimacy, because Mr Eight will insist upon taking his petty grievances and irrational jealousies to bed with him. Instead of being an ardent lover he's more likely to play the role of Spanish inquisitor.

He is often rather cold and undemonstrative and he has difficulty in expressing emotion. Miss Seven, however, is emotional and passionate and could find his moodiness very trying. Fortunately she is also a reasonable, understanding woman so perhaps, given time, they will be able to reach a working compromise in this particular area of their relationship. At the end of the day this combination is really a case of mind over matter — her spiritual enlightenment over his materialism.

Male Eight:Female Eight

An 8:8 combination is always something of a gamble and it is anyone's guess how it will develop. When two Eights decide to co-operate with each other the result is a well-organized, dynamic team which is completely unstoppable. But Eight is a number of extremes and reversals. Once that element of competition is allowed to creep into their relationship the outcome could be disastrous. They need to handle their combined strength with care, respect and kid gloves if they don't want to destroy each other.

Mr Eight is strong, tough and practical and his partner is much the same. They both want to succeed in life and be seen to have done so. These two set the standards that everyone else tries to live up to. They work tirelessly and relentlessly to accomplish their objectives. They seek status, recognition and wealth. Nothing else like happiness, peace of mind or higher feelings seems to interest them in the slightest. They are a mercenary couple of social climbers who have no other values in life other than purely material ones.

Both are charming, poised and dignified on the surface, but when the pressure is on they are both capable of selfishness, aggression and tyranny. They have hides like elephants and hair-trigger tempers. Provided they work together towards a common goal all will be well. But if one steps out of line or has big ideas of his or her own, the ensuing explosion could reach nuclear proportions. Eight is the number of struggle and tenacity; of obstinacy and ruthlessness; this relationship could go either way and an Eight's failures can be just as spectacular as his successes.

Perhaps there won't be much going on between them as far as intimacy is concerned because Eights are often cold and undemonstrative. Affection is something they always have difficulty with and their moods can go from the sublime to the ridiculous in a matter of seconds. They are brusque and detached one moment and gentle and sympathetic the next. In love they are loyal and devoted but this rarely has a chance to show as they're usually far too busy being jealous and possessive. They both need constant reassurance of fidelity and will probably while away their intimate moments checking up on each other or trying to catch each other out instead of getting on with the real business in hand. It's a game at which they are both masters and one which somehow they seem to enjoy in a strange, perverted way.

Male Eight:Female Nine

Mr Eight and Miss Nine are on two completely different wavelengths, their numbers are in conflict (one even, one odd) and their aims and ambitions are poles apart. But for some inexplicable reason there are good chances for them to succeed. What's more, they seem to bring out the best in each other. Mr Eight is practical and can offer stability while Miss Nine is a visionary and can contribute unusual ideas. Provided Mr Eight doesn't become too domineering and Miss Nine doesn't do anything foolhardy they could have a lifetime of happiness ahead of them.

Mr Eight has an innate desire to succeed in life and is well equipped to do so. He is truthful, reliable, practical and always honours his obligations. He is strong, tough, imaginative and knowledgeable. He seeks not only money but also social recognition and although his path through life is seldom an easy one, he never lets obstacles and disappointments get him down — few self-made men ever do. He will work flat out, day and night if necessary, when he feels it will get him somewhere. He does tend to let his forceful nature get the better of him from time to time especially when working under pressure. Then he becomes hard, selfish and utterly ruthless. He is cool, calm, collected and charming but beneath the surface lies a deep, very intense nature indeed. He finds emotion difficult to express, except anger, and usually hides his feelings lest they somehow colour his judgement. He is not the easiest of men to live with but, there again, Miss Nine does love a challenge.

Miss Nine is large-minded, idealistic and full of compassion for anyone who is being oppressed or downtrodden. She has an intense urge to serve in a worthwhile cause but may be intolerant if opposed (Mr Eight please note). She is determined, active and courageous as well as imaginative, creative and susceptible to unpredictable flashes of inspiration. She has a clear, quick mind, which can sometimes get her into hot water when she acts impulsively, a fighting spirit and a hasty temper. She is honest, trusting, independent and loyal; strongly resents criticism; values friendship; can compromise with humour and disagree without rancour. She is resourceful, a good organizer and really an exceptional, charming person. Mr Eight should be proud to share his life with her and should treat her with the respect and admiration she undoubtedly deserves. She has grit, will-power and strength. United these two people stand together, divided they are very much on their own.

Mr Eight can be a moody, undemonstrative man to share a bed with and to make matters worse he is jealous. He sees imaginary rivals lurking behind every half-open wardrobe door and always wants to know who was on the telephone when the call wasn't for him. He is subject to great extremes of emotion which makes him unpredictable and difficult to gauge at times. Miss Nine is passionate, romantic and still very impulsive. She never seeks occasions for arguments but if he rejects her too often she can be a difficult woman to handle once she's angry. Although she will try to follow her partner's wishes in most things, this deep, intense man will certainly put her patience to the test. These two have a few initial problems to iron out but after that they shouldn't experience any further insuperable difficulties.

Male Nine:Female One

There can be little doubt that this combination will prosper because together Mr Nine and Miss One possess a touch of genius. Mr Nine has integrity, which tempers his partner's creative flair, and his wisdom acts as a sounding-board for her often brilliant ideas. Miss One, on the other hand, is a pioneer, a woman who will show him the way to enter new fields of expression and who is, intellectually, his equal. However, neither is perfect. He can be intolerant when he feels he's being opposed or criticized while she can be equally stubborn and bossy. These negative traits must be kept in check if squabbles and arguments are to be avoided.

Nine is a mystical number which represents mental and spiritual supremacy. Mr Nine is large-minded, visionary and idealistic. He has an intense urge to serve in a worthy cause and earnestly desires to improve human life in order to make the world a better place in which to live. In fact, he's a 'do-gooder' through and through but never in a sycophantic, interfering way. There's nothing 'holier than thou' about his attitude; he's sincere, honest, trusting and sympathetic. He has a clear, quick mind, a great imagination and a genuine love of humanity. He is an exceptionally strong character; courageous, independent, resourceful and determined. From a negative point of view he is rather quick-tempered and tends to see everything on a global scale with the result that he often fails to recognize the needs and feelings of those closest to him. But his worst fault, and his greatest danger, lies in impulsiveness. His foolhardiness could get him into trouble at times and he is also likely to be accident prone. He's a good organizer and a man who needs to be in control. He likes to be looked up to and indeed recognized as head of his household. This could cause a few domestic problems because Miss One will automatically assume that *she* is.

Miss One is no shy violet; she's a giant sunflower who likes to bask in warmth and light. She is ambitious, single-minded, self-reliant and far more interested in following her career than she is in playing the role of housewife or mother. She is positive, active, daring and purposeful. She knows her own mind; needs neither encouragement nor advice from others and, once decided on a course of action, cannot be diverted from her chosen path. Miss One tackles responsibilities unflinchingly, has the capacity to adjust to almost any circumstances and is generally popular and the focus of attention. She is charming, attractive, affectionate and sincere, with impatience and obstinacy as her failings. She is generous and forgiving; usually reasonable in her attitude and, like Mr Nine, has the ability to compromise and the magnanimity to end an argument. These two have much in common and theirs is a relationship which won't require miracles to make it work — only a little faith and a good portion of common sense.

As a lover Mr Nine can be very exciting. He is romantic, passionate, impulsive and extremely persuasive. He's neither jealous nor possessive but rather conceited about his prowess so if Miss One has any criticisms to level at his performance she had better choose her words with care — he has a hasty temper. Miss One is inventive, adventurous and always prepared to try something different. She is never afraid to take the initiative and will probably have plenty of ideas which she wants to put to the test. She is confident, demonstrative, active and original but always completely in control of herself and the situation. Bedtime sounds like fun-time for these two sexual athletes and a few early nights are to be recommended.

Male Nine:Female Two

Imagination, vision, insight, stability and understanding all exist to some extent within this relationship. Miss Two is receptive, sensitive and submissive and because her partner is such an inspiring, stimulating man she is easily influenced by his mental and spiritual supremacy. Together they should achieve balance, harmony and peace of mind. The Visionary (Nine) and The Sensitive (Two) can usually rise above the earthly plane — their thoughts are often of higher, finer things. These two represent a true marriage of minds as well as the purely physical union that takes place when two creative people decide to join forces and spend their lives together. Their relationship is very special and will undoubtedly stand the test of time.

Mr Nine's goal in life is to show others the right way to live through his breadth of thinking and to promote universal love. He is patient and understanding, lives up to his ideals and is always ready to help others less fortunate than himself. He genuinely cares about humanity and has an intense urge to serve in a worthwhile cause which could benefit mankind. He is active, courageous and determined, makes an excellent leader and a first class organizer. He is honest, trusting, perceptive and enterprising. He has a clear, quick mind, great imagination and is susceptible to the odd, unpredictable flash of intuition.

He is always prepared to fight for what he wants and is usually successful because he has grit, an iron will and tremendous staying power. But he can be intolerant when opposed, insensitive to the needs of his loved ones when involved in some particularly far-reaching enterprise, hasty in temper and impulsive in word and deed. Impulsiveness is probably his worst fault, and perhaps his greatest danger; many Nines are accident prone and there's no reason to believe he should be any different. But, by and large, he is a capable, caring man with wide sympathies and great charm.

Two is a neutral number which is easily influenced and for this reason Miss Two is hesitant, indecisive and subject to frequent changes of mind. She's also rather shy and self-conscious, always preferring to follow rather than to lead. She's quiet, even-tempered, modest and conciliatory. But please don't go thinking she's grey and amorphous. There is more to Miss Two than meets the eye and rather like an iceberg seven eighths of her character lies hidden beneath the surface. She is creative, imaginative and artistic; humorous, sharp-witted and a fascinating conversationalist. She is adaptable, cheerful, persuasive, resourceful, sociable and inventive but sadly not very forceful in carrying out her ideas. She does have a black side and her moods and emotions seem to fluctuate from one day to the next. She is also jealous and possessive but most of her suffering in this direction is usually of the self-inflicted variety. The majority of the time she's a pleasant, good-natured person but when her moon is on the wane she can be intensely irritating.

In the privacy of their own home Mr Nine is romantic, passionate and impulsive. When he suddenly decides he's in an amorous mood the gardening, washing up or anything else will have to wait. His partner is also a romantic, emotional woman although at times he will need to be extra-persuasive especially when she's feeling a bit down or depressed. These two should be blissfully happy provided her negativity doesn't get out of hand and spoil everything they've created.

Male Nine:Female Three

At face value this 9:3 combination looks like a rewarding relationship. Firstly both numbers are odd and Mr Nine and Miss Three have a great deal in common. They both have clear, quick minds as well as imagination, artistic flair and adaptable natures but somehow this mixture of talents and personalities never quite gels and the initial promise of their relationship sometimes fails to come to fruition. Mr Nine is always wanting to save the world and Miss Three won't take his schemes seriously. They are both impulsive, although luck usually favours her, and she is also inclined to be bossy which only encourages his hasty temper.

Mr Nine is a visionary and has a genuine love of humanity which he is always trying to serve. He wants to improve human life and better conditions on a global scale. He's large-minded, active, courageous and independent. He will always fight for what he wants and because he has grit, will-power and the determination to succeed he usually gets there in the end. He is honest, trusting and loyal; enterprising, imaginative and idealistic. He's resourceful and a good organizer but strongly resents criticism because, although not actually conceited, he does hold a high opinion of himself. He only has one major fault which is his impulsiveness. It often lands him in trouble particularly when he does something rash or speaks out of turn. He is quite likely to be accident prone.

For the most part, however, Mr Nine is a charming, sympathetic character. However, Miss Three may not agree with this as these two manage to rub each other up the wrong way. Either he'll get the wrong end of the stick completely or she will find fault with what he's trying to say. This relationship seems to have its own built-in self-destruct mechanism and unfortunately neither realizes just what will trigger the whole thing off until it is far too late.

Miss Three is witty, lively and versatile. She is talented and creative, expressing herself boldly and vividly. She's one of those people who can concentrate on several different things at a time and still do them all competently. In fact she has a very fine brain, a satirical sense of humour and the infuriating habit of running mental rings around everyone. She has to be one jump ahead and this often causes friction between her and

Mr Nine because women that are too clever play havoc with his ego. Miss Three likes to do her own thing in her own way and, although she could never be described as a loner, she does find that partnerships cramp her flamboyant style. She's also proud, independent, dislikes being under obligation and chafes under the least restraint. Like her symbol the otter, she's a free spirit who loses all her sparkle and brilliance in captivity. Self-expression is of the utmost importance to her but Mr Nine rarely realizes this.

Strangely enough the physical side of their relationship should run like well-oiled clockwork despite all their differences of opinion. And like a well-tended timepiece their lovemaking never seems to stop or even slow down. Mr Nine is romantic, passionate and impulsive while she's easy-going, sensual and very much given to spur-of-the-moment gestures.

Male Nine:Female Four

If you're looking for a dynamic, high-speed couple you certainly won't find them here. They make all their movements at a sedate, leisurely pace. And there's a reason for this; they both have much to teach and indeed show each other so why hurry and spoil things? This combination will be around for a long time and neither has the slightest intention of forcing matters. Mr Nine can help the down-to-earth Miss Four develop her latent spirituality while she can pass on many practical skills that he would not otherwise acquire. This couple have all the time in the world.

Nine is a mystical number which stands for mental and spiritual supremacy; hope and achievement; intuition and inspiration and it comes as no surprise to discover that Mr Nine is large-minded, visionary and idealistic. His goal in life is to promote universal love and harmony and he achieves this by being patient, understanding and compassionate. He needs to be of service to others and has an inborn urge to serve in a worthwhile cause. He has a clear, quick mind, great imagination and very big ideas which occasionally stand in the way of everything else that is important to him. He is determined, active and courageous; trusting, trustworthy and totally honest. Impulsiveness is his main fault, with intolerance and irritability coming very close behind. He values friendship, is neither jealous nor possessive and is generally able to compromise with humour and disagree without rancour. He's an educated teacher who will do his utmost to improve Miss Four's mind and to elevate her thoughts away from purely mundane matters.

Four is the number of foundation; of dullness, endurance and stability. Miss Four is a very basic woman; she's solid, reliable and extremely well-organized. She is good with money, especially when it comes to balancing her books, hard-working, energetic and respectable. She never gives up even when the going gets tough, faces up to all her responsibilities and handles problems calmly and with confidence. But what Mr Nine admires most about her is the fact that, deep down, she has a secret desire to alleviate poverty and suffering which is very much in tune with his own desire for massive global reforms. She is very positive and, at times, unconventional in her views and opinions. If there's a good cause to support or a lame dog to befriend she will be first in line to help. Stolid and humourless she might be but her heart's in the right place — and it's big. She has her faults but they are fairly harmless and seem to hurt her more than they do other people. She is sensitive, her feelings are easily wounded and she can become rather melancholy and despondent when her plans haven't been quite so successful as she had hoped. Miss Four is a good, steady woman who will bring balance and perspective into Mr Nine's big, wide, demanding world.

Don't expect any wild orgies or sultry nights of passion from them because the slow, leisurely pace of the relationship pervades even this couple's lovemaking. Mr Nine is romantic, tender and perceptive. He gauges his partner's moods instinctively and knows exactly what approach to make and when. Miss Four is not an adventurous woman and although she is faithful, sentimental and considerate she does like some order in her lovemaking, as in everything else. She doesn't want sudden, mad urges or strange invitations; it's the tried and trusted for her and provided Mr Nine keeps his impulsive streak under firm control these two won't go far wrong.

Male Nine:Female Five

Mr Nine and Miss Five are like a pair of magnets which can attract or repel depending entirely upon polarity. Initially, when their feelings for each other are at their most positive, they get along fine but as time goes by and their attitudes begin to show a distinct change, negativity slowly creeps into their relationship until finally a complete about face seems to have been performed: the two magnets now try to forcibly drive each other away. In other words Mr Nine and Miss Five have become 'poles apart' and unless they are both prepared to make a superhuman effort to restore the balance they will remain unthinking, uncaring and totally unconcerned about each other.

Mr Nine is a man of high mental and spiritual achievement. He's certainly no fool, even though he does behave like one at times, especially where his partner is concerned. He has a clear, quick mind, great imagination, high ideals and a genuine love of humanity which he earnestly wishes to serve; and this is where this couple's problems really begin. He very often becomes so obsessed with trying to put the world to rights that he completely ignores the needs and feelings of those closest to him and Miss Five isn't a lady who can put up with being ignored.

Mr Nine is capable of exerting great influence over others. He is determined, active and courageous; will fight for what he wants and stand up for what he believes in. His faults are impulsiveness, intolerance and obstinacy coupled with a hasty temper. He and Miss Five will often fight. To most people he seems to be an understanding, compassionate, charming man, but to Miss Five he can be like a red rag to a bull.

Miss Five is an individualist. She is restless, clever and impatient. She's an extremely astute woman who seldom wastes her time on unrealistic schemes and enterprises. She is talented, original and creative. In fact she does so many things well that her main problem in life is her ability to discriminate. She seems attracted by everything (including the magnetic Mr Nine) but held by little. She is adventurous; loves to explore new places and investigate new ideas; hates to feel in a rut and is always prepared to take risks sometimes just for the sheer hell of it. She is highly strung, impulsive, quick in thought and decision and always on the look-out for some excitement. She, like Mr Nine, can be irritable and quick-tempered but in her case it's because she burns the candle at both ends. Miss Five is an exciting, fun person to have around but once she starts getting bored with a relationship she thinks about flying off to a sunnier climate, like her symbol, the swallow. She values her freedom and an earnest 'do-gooder' is the last person she'll want to get bogged down with for long.

Undoubtedly the best aspect of this combination, and perhaps the only thing that keeps it going, is the pleasure and happiness they experience in each others arms. When these two kiss and make up it can be quite an occasion, but unfortunately their truces seldom last for long. Mr Nine is romantic, passionate and impulsive; he's full of surprises and that's just what Miss Five likes. She is ruled by the number of pure sexuality and with her it's often a case of anything goes provided her partner is a consenting adult. She's sensual, demanding, occasionally selfish and always prepared to make the first move if necessary. If only these two tempestuous lovers could apply the formula they use in private to the rest of their relationship then life would be much happier for both of them.

Male Nine:Female Six

This duo can look forward to harmony and balance. Their relationship is built on beauty (Six) and truth (Nine). Mr Nine and Miss Six instinctively know how to give and take at all levels and a partnership such as this rarely comes to grief. The visionary Mr Nine contributes inspiration and high ideals while the peacemaking Miss Six creates a tranquil atmosphere in which their relationship can take root and grow. They seldom run into trouble and any problems they do encounter are soon resolved in a friendly, equable manner.

Nine is the highest of all the Love Number vibrations and Mr Nine is a man of great mental and spiritual achievement. He has wide sympathies, great charm and an intense urge to serve a worthwhile cause. He's intuitive and far-sighted; imaginative and inspiring; influential and resourceful. He strongly resents criticism, especially of his artistic endeavours; rebels against any kind of interference and has a rather quick temper. However, he can usually manage to compromise with humour.

Mr Nine has a strong will, tremendous determination and an innate desire to be master of his own fate. He likes to be looked up to and recognized as head of his own household so it's a good thing Miss Six isn't a militant feminist or they would almost certainly fall out. Perhaps his worst fault and probably his greatest danger lies in his impulsiveness which tends to make him accident prone. He needs to work on this and should try to think before he speaks.

Miss Six is a delightful woman with a talent for home and family life. She is idealistic, imaginative and usually at her best when involved in some kind of creative activity. She's a born home-maker and surrounds herself with unusual ornaments and tasteful paintings. She is also a born hostess and likes nothing better than to entertain family and friends in her comfortable home. She is well balanced, open-minded, self-controlled and extremely intelligent. She loathes discord or jealousy and all she really asks from life is to be able to make everyone around her feel happy and secure. Miss Six has the rare gift of intuitively understanding the needs and difficulties of others and somehow she manages to bring out the best in even the most unlikely people. She's a just, kind, courageous woman and an ideal partner for Mr Nine.

In the privacy of their bedroom this couple are not particularly adventurous but this doesn't mean that their lovemaking is dull or routine. Together they are a very spiritual couple whose minds demand more attention than their bodies. During moments of intimacy they are able to experience happiness and fulfilment on two different levels of consciousness at one and the same time.

Mr Nine is a patient, understanding, romantic lover who is on some occasions prompted to act by impulse while on others driven by passion. He's loyal, sympathetic and honest. Jealousy is something which rarely troubles him but he can be difficult if his suspicions are aroused. Miss Six is neither overtly jealous nor maddeningly possessive and she too tends to the romantic and ideal in all matters of love. She's warm, affectionate and loyal but hers is more like mother love than the sensual. This combination rarely experiences any insuperable physical problems.

Male Nine:Female Seven

Spirituality is all very well if it is kept in perspective but Mr Nine and Miss Seven are a little too 'airy-fairy' for their own good. If they don't watch out they could be in real danger of totally losing touch with reality. They can achieve peace, harmony and perfect understanding within their relationship but it is not of this world.

Mr Nine is animated by his soul, his finer feelings and his obsession to serve humanity in a worthwhile cause. Money is of little interest to him. He is large-minded, visionary and idealistic with wide sympathies and even greater understanding. He's an inspiring, stimulating man who is capable of exerting tremendous influence over not only other people but also his whole environment. He has a fine brain, a wonderful imagination and a genuine love of mankind. He's always prepared to fight for what is right, never gives up when the going gets difficult and usually ends up having his own way in most things. Like his partner Miss Seven, he has powers of ESP and is also given to unpredictable flashes of pure inspiration. He does have faults — a hasty temper, insensitivity at times and a stubborn streak but these are all far outweighed by his absolute plethora of positive characteristics. When a man ruled by the mystical number (Nine) decides to enter into a personal relationship with a woman ruled by the magic number (Seven) the combination is almost supernatural.

Miss Seven is intellectual, philosophical and secretive. She has a brilliant, questioning mind and because she's unable to accept conventional theories and explanations she uses it to explore the world about her in search of truths concerning the nature and meaning of existence. Material requirements seem unimportant to her but she does need to be left alone at times to reflect and meditate as this is essential for her inner growth. Her imaginative and intuitive powers are extremely advanced and these tend to carry her far beyond the bounds of rationality into a world peopled entirely by her own day-dream and fantasies. She has peculiar ideas about religion, a great leaning to the occult and she is artistic, dignified and knowledgeable.

Mr Nine is romantic, passionate and impulsive. Miss Seven is emotional, demonstrative and very demanding. On a purely physical level the appetites and desires of both partners seem well matched and with this combination what goes on behind their locked bedroom door is probably best left to the imagination.

Male Nine:Female Eight

A combination of Mr Nine and Miss Eight isn't so much a personal relationship as a war of attrition. Day by day, week after week they wear each other down by a steady process of harassment, friction and abrasion until the very foundations on which they hoped to build a future have been completely eroded. Why they got together is a great numerological mystery because Mr Nine is always too busy rushing around trying to help everyone else except Miss Eight, while she sets her sights high on a life of luxury and, of course, social status. But it never comes as a surprise when they split up.

Mr Nine is spiritual, visionary and idealistic. He is one of life's 'do-gooders' with an innate desire to serve in a worthwhile cause and a genuine love of humanity to go with it. He often becomes so prepossessed with trying to make the world a better place that he appears blinkered. He has a high opinion of himself and his worth; strongly resents criticisms; becomes intolerant if opposed; brooks no interference with his plans and demands to be looked up to and recognized as head of the house. Miss Eight certainly won't stand for this. Somehow she seems to bring out the worst in him. He has a hasty temper and she is bound to feel the rough edge of his tongue from time to time. The picture so far doesn't look very rosy and is not likely to improve.

Miss Eight is mercenary and materialistic. She is strong, tough and practical but when coupled with Mr Nine she appears hard, selfish and tyrannical. She regards a certain amount of argument within a relationship as par for the course, and is quite likely to give as good as she gets. She is ambitious and craves money, power and worldly involvement, not the mental and spiritual supremacy her partner strives so hard to achieve. Miss Eight is self-disciplined, unscrupulous and ruthless. Her knowledge is gained from experience not textbooks and her determination to succeed comes straight from the heart. When ruled by the number Eight there can never be a happy medium — no shades of grey. Eights will do tremendously well or they will fail miserably.

For as long as the relationship lasts it will almost certainly be a case of separate bedrooms in mind if not body. Mr Nine is a romantic, passionate lover but even between the sheets he probably won't please his partner. Miss Eight has great difficulty expressing her feelings and is subject to swings of emotion from cool and detached one moment to provocative the next. It's small wonder Mr Nine never knows where he stands and hardly surprising that he very soon gives up trying to find out.

Male Nine:Female Nine

Nine is the highest of all the Love Number vibrations and stands not only especially if it's novel, interesting and on a grand scale, couldn't possibly fail. Neither is afraid of hard work or long hours, they both handle responsibility seriously and no problem could possibly be big enough for mental and spiritual supremacy but also hope, achievement and inspiration. It is the mystical number and all those ruled by it are very special individuals. A combination of two Nines only serves to double its powers and represents perhaps the ultimate in relationships.

Wisdom, knowledge and imagination are all to be found here and this couple could do much to benefit humanity for which they care passionately. They are perfectly balanced, perfectly matched and will almost certainly remain together, peacefully and harmoniously, in this life and, knowing them, quite probably into the next as well.

All Nines are basically alike so when describing Mr Nine we describe Miss Nine as well. Mr Nine is a visionary. He has undeniable charm, wide sympathies and a clear, quick mind. He is resourceful, stimulating and capable of exerting great influence over other people and, indeed, his whole environment. He is artistic, instinctive and at times amusingly eccentric, especially in his later years. He's given to the odd, unpredictable flashes of inspiration which border on genius.

Mr Nine is honest, trusting and loyal as well as being a good organizer and a patient teacher. He's a fighter in all he attempts and because he has will-power, grit and determination he generally takes obstacles and set-backs in his massive stride.

Now we come to his faults. Mr Nine tends to get so wrapped up in his grand schemes to benefit humanity that he somehow fails to notice the needs and feelings of those nearest to him. He also rebels against interference, strongly resents criticism, may be intolerant if opposed and has a hasty temper. But perhaps his greatest fault is impulsiveness. His hasty words and actions often land him in trouble and are frequently the cause of minor accidents and injuries.

In general terms Mr Nine is an exceptional, broad-minded man; full of compassion for those in trouble and always ready to advise those with problems. And the same goes for Miss Nine. A combination such as this could set the world to rights given time and opportunity.

This couple rarely experience physical or emotional problems within their relationship simply because they are in complete agreement on all levels of consciousness. All Nines are romantic, passionate and impulsive and when love, understanding and absolute devotion are added the picture seems complete. This 9:9 combination is probably the closest any couple can get to 'the perfect relationship' and even then they only fall short of the maximum possible score by a mere fraction. They should be blissfully happy, completely fulfilled and will set a shining example for everyone else to try and emulate. They are the highest and last of all the possible Love Number combinations.

CHAPTER FOUR

General Relationships

The art of using Love Number comparisons to reveal compatability isn't just limited to people. If you want to see what your prospects for promotion are like you can simply compare your own number with the number of the company you work for.

And if you are an employer and want to know if a potential employee fits in with your company image, you can do the same.

A company's number is calculated from the date that it was first registered. But if it's not possible to pinpoint the precise date there is another method.

Simply write out the name of the business and follow the method given for finding Life Numbers in Chapter Five. The Life Number alone won't give you the complete picture but it will give you a reasonable outline of the firm in question.

One:One

A One with a One can only be described as a powerful and potentially dangerous combination because they are both born leaders. Unless they are prepared to work as a team, trouble could easily arise.

Ones are overtly aggressive. In order to maintain a reasonably peaceful coexistence they would both have to learn how to co-operate and perhaps even draw up a special agreement setting out exactly who does what — and stick to it. Even this would have to be handled with great care so that neither one felt that they were, in any way, playing second fiddle to the other.

But if two Ones manage to reach a working agreement their venture, especially if it's novel, interesting and on a grand scale, couldn't possibly fail. Neither is afraid of hard work or long hours, they both handle responsibility seriously and no problem could possibly be big enough to stop two Ones who are heading for success. They could overcome any obstacle between them — either by fair means or foul. They wouldn't even have to like each other particularly, as long as they both respected the other's judgement. And Ones are superb judges of just about everything except their own egos. If a careful balance of power is resolutely maintained a partnership like this could go far.

When a Number One employee works for a Number One company this promises to be a successful combination for all concerned. One is a go-ahead number so for a pioneering person working for a progressive company the chances of rising to a high position look very good indeed.

On the home front, when there is more than one Number One child in a family a good deal of sibling rivalry could ensue with each child trying to outdo the other and wanting more attention than everyone else put together, with the squabbles growing fiercer and more heated as the two warring factions battle on towards maturity. When a One:One combination consists of adult and child, however, the problems will be less serious at first as the adult will always have the final say although the adolescent years could prove something of a minefield for all concerned as the younger One starts to feel his/her feet and decides that it's time to issue a challenge.

One:Two

One plus Two equals a highly successful combination because what one lacks, the other can provide. They complement each other perfectly. One comes up with all the ideas whilst Two contributes the talent and ability needed to carry them out.

One is the go-getter who wants to be firmly in control of the situation. He or she is ambitious, aggressive, impatient and, at times, downright bossy while Two is the complete opposite. Twos are shy and retiring, preferring to follow rather than to lead but despite their lack of drive they are nobody's fools. They are observant, shrewd and highly intuitive. While One is busy making a big impression on everyone, Two is quietly observing the whole performance and summing up the situation from a distance. Ones think big and act big, they need to see and be seen. They want to do all the interesting and exciting parts in any enterprise so when a Two comes along and is perfectly happy to take care of all the mundane tasks, One can hardly believe his luck. Two never challenges One's authority, never questions decisions and never gets in his way. A One:Two relationship means that both parties can be themselves while at the same time forming a highly organized and stress-free team. Differences rarely crop up between them except on the odd occasion when One manages to hurt the sensitive Two's feelings with a thoughtless remark or when Two dithers too long over something rather unusual that One wants him to do.

When a Number One is employed by a Company Number Two he could prove to be a very valuable asset indeed because he's hard-working, innovative and responsible. He is also overtly ambitious so by keeping his company's interests at heart and generating new opportunities for them, the chances for his own advancement should also greatly increase. From his point of view a Two Company is ideal because it can provide the financial backing he so needs to promote his ideas. It is no use Number One inventing new machinery or devising novel ways round old problems if no one is prepared to put his ideas to good use — and a Two Company certainly would because they need a man with brains and foresight.

Conversely, when a Number Two works for a Company Number One the outlook is just as good. The employers are bound to have enough chiefs but indians are in short supply. They need people to keep the books, administrators, despatch clerks, secretaries; and these jobs are just what a Two does best. He is unlikely to push for promotion but will work steadily, unobtrusively and honestly at his job and everyone will be happy — or will they? Twos need stability and they might feel that a company which is forever trying something new, and therefore not guaranteed to succeed, cannot offer them the long-term security they so desire. They could well get cold feet and turn down the offer of a job with a Company Number One.

In a family environment Ones and Twos should all get along very well together because their needs and interests rarely conflict. The only time real problems arise is when a Number One parent begins to despair of their Number Two offspring's lack of ambition and reluctance to decide on a career. Then the parent could, if not careful, be tempted to push the child in the direction they think best, which would be wrong for all concerned.

One:Three

Materially this could be a very rewarding combination because when a One and a Three decide to pull together they can accomplish almost anything provided that One does nothing too impetuous and that Three learns to keep his mind on the matter in hand.

Ones always tend to lead the way in any situation but become even more aggressive when pursuing financial rewards. They are full of wonderful new plans to put to the test and always seeking some new slant which would revolutionize an old angle. They are the innovators and will bring to this partnership more than enough ideas for the Three to develop.

Threes are versatile and brilliant. They have the ability to concentrate on more than one thing at a time much to the infuriation of others. They too are ambitious, power-loving and well organized but don't make quite such a song and dance about it as a Number One. Threes are persuasive, talented and learn quickly. You only have to tell them once and they understand immediately.

All the right ingredients for success can be found within a One:Three partnership. One just has to set the ball rolling and Three will know exactly how to present, package, market and generate the right sort of interest to make the product or idea a winner. However, if personalities are allowed to creep in it could be an entirely different story.

Number One must learn to curb his bossiness and take advice. He should also try to think on a slightly smaller scale than he usually does and resist the temptation to leap before he looks. Three must learn to take everything more seriously and not be so fiercely independent. With his quick mind, he can run rings around most people if he chooses, but he should take care not to do it too often as no one likes to appear a fool, especially not a One and definitely not in front of others.

When a One is employed by a Company Number Three he will certainly have plenty to offer although he may not be adaptable enough for all their needs. Three is the number of versatility and unless he can change his ideas to fit in with their schemes he may find he is useful in only one of the many areas that the company operates. A Three, on the other hand, can make himself at home almost anywhere especially if he is employed by a Company Number One. Ones want to lead the way in their own particular field and need people with quick minds, artistic flair and undeniable talent to handle advertising, public relations, marketing and so on. A Three would fit the bill perfectly.

Ones and Threes should coexist in reasonable harmony within a family environment except for the occasional squabble when One, as usual, gets too big for his boots and Three decides to cut him down to size with a sarcastic remark. Even when the children reach maturity a One parent should be able to come up with some useful plans which a younger Three could use. And, indeed, a Three parent would undoubtedly be able to advise a One child how to put his talents to the best possible use because Threes always know how to develop good ideas.

One:Four

This combination works marginally better on a business footing than at very close quarters because One and Four often find each other very exasperating. Ones often act impulsively and this is something a Four simply never does and therefore cannot understand. Fours are cautious by nature and extremely circumspect about everything they do. A Four would never dream of making a move without a great deal of careful consideration. So both people concerned in a One:Four relationship will need to make a conscious effort if they seriously want this alliance to make any progress.

The One partner must slow down and set a steadier pace otherwise the Four could find it extremely difficult to keep abreast of developments. The One must be more patient, less demanding, not quite so stubborn and, on occasion, prepared to explain his actions. He will probably fight against this as Ones never like having to account for themselves and feel that their authority should be unquestionable.

Number Four will also have to make some adjustments to his outlook and could start by developing a more flexible attitude to life. He must learn to be more adaptable and to bend with the circumstances rather than trying to create a routine which fits in with his requirements. He also has the perverse habit of viewing everything from the opposite angle to everyone else which could cause problems in this One/Four combination. A One instinctively knows he's right and doesn't care what other people think so he certainly won't want to hear Four's quaint views on any subject. These two must both be prepared to make sacrifices if they honestly want to achieve something positive from this partnership.

When a One is employed by a Company Number Four his chances of success within such an environment don't look very promising. The company is, in all probability, an old family firm which has been painstakingly built up over several generations by tried and tested methods. They're not in business to get rich quick, won't be looking to cut corners and certainly won't be in the market for go-ahead new ideas. They like things just the way they are and for this reason they don't really need a One with his aggressive approach and burning ambitions.

The reverse of this situation looks much the same for a Four. A go-ahead Company One needs men of vision and ideas for their key positions not safe and sure Fours. He, on the other hand, might feel that the company lacks stability. A One Company could well go into liquidation overnight if they failed to see a return on the capital invested in some new venture and this constant uncertainty could prove too much for a Four to cope with for any length of time.

Within a family, Ones and Fours of any sex or age group rarely manage to see eye to eye. Unlike Ones, Fours are basically unadventurous and have no desire to do anything remotely new or exciting. Monotonous, old-fashioned games simply don't appeal to a One and there is really nothing of common interest for them to share with a Four brother or sister. In a parent/child relationship, Ones and Fours still don't really get along as the One child is too much of an enigma, not to mention a handful, for the Four parent to cope with. And a Four child never really does anything out of the ordinary for the One parent to be proud of. In fact any attempts on their part to push the child usually end in tears. In general terms Fours and Ones have too many insurmountable differences between them for this to be anything but a middling combination.

One:Five

Versatility could be the saving grace in a One:Five combination. One and Five are very changeable numbers so you would both need to be able to adapt quickly and readily to cope with each other's demands. However, if you are prepared to accept the challenge (and we all know that Fives are not afraid to take the occasional risk) you could do very well in partnership together because you have a lot to offer.

Before we decide what adjustments will be necessary let's first see what you have in common. On the positive side you are both adventurous, capable, original, creative and clever while from a negative viewpoint you're both obstinate, impatient, inconsiderate and impulsive. Already we can see some possible trouble spots to watch out for especially if you can't agree over something.

As far as adjustments are concerned, One, as usual, must try not to be too aggressive in his desire to lead. He should try not to show resentment if Five has a few good ideas of his own to contribute and he must learn to share. He's got to realize that in any partnership he can't have all the glory for himself.

Five also has some flaws in his character which will need to be kept in close check especially in this partnership where he is likely to come up against some strong opposition from his One partner. Sarcasm has no place here because One can give as good as he gets; neither is there room for conceit and above all he must realize that he can't leave a job half finished, as he's often inclined to do, because One will see to it that he doesn't.

A One working for a Five Company could rise to great heights provided that he or she can weather the storms that are likely to blow up from time to time.

A Five employed by a One Company may find the situation somewhat difficult because, although he has excellent qualifications, he's easily bored and no organization is going to put up with someone who wants to be on the move all the time. However, if his job incorporates travel then he will be perfectly happy to move around within the company or on their behalf. Five is also the number of sexuality so he'll have to keep a tight rein on his base instincts as an office romance that goes wrong could spoil his chances for promotion — especially if it's with the boss's daughter.

In the home Ones and Fives will inevitably have their share of ups and downs because they are so alike in many ways. But a competitive spirit between children of these numbers should, in the long run, bring out the best in both of them. Eventually they will learn to share, co-operate and, when necessary, agree to differ. Five parents shouldn't experience too many difficulties with One offspring, even in their late teens, but when the situation is reversed a Five's desire to leave home and travel could cause some problems.

One:Six

A joint business venture between a One and a Six has all the hallmarks for success provided there is sufficient scope for the Six to be creative. He has an artistic flair and always needs to have an outlet for his talent. This shouldn't cause any problems here because the One partner really only wants to manage and control and this would leave the Six free to pursue his own particular interests within the partnership.

Sixes are far more than merely artistic, they are well-balanced, resourceful, courageous and magnetic. They are also rather good at handling people which in business is a distinct advantage. They have the uncanny knack of being able to get the best out of almost anyone without appearing to have brought any undue pressure to bear. Money isn't particularly important to them — One can handle that side of things — although Sixes could seldom be described as wasteful or extravagant. However, they do have a darker side to their usually kind and sympathetic natures and, if roused, they can be just as stubborn, domineering and intractable as any One.

Ones resent advice and often refuse to follow it. They also dislike restraint in whatever form it might take, so if Six should attempt to make any kindly suggestions or try to steer One away from a potentially disastrous course of action he will be wasting his time. Ones, however, do have retentive memories, a great capacity for hard work and the ability to overcome obstacles and endure hardships without complaint — all admirable qualities which they would contribute to a One:Six partnership.

A Six Company would probably be involved in public service or the arts so a One employee stands a very good chance of rising rapidly to a position of control within such an organization for the simple reason that he's a good organizer, he's efficient and much more down to earth, when it comes to handling finances, than any 'arty' Six type. What's more, he is also rather creative, in a novel sort of way, so his ideas could well be put to good use by a Six company.

A Six engaged by a One company could get on just as well. Public relations, personnel, advertising and design are all areas in which he could excel and are all, fortunately, departments for which a One has no particular talent.

In the home Ones and Sixes shouldn't cause too many problems when young. Six is the number of peace and harmony. However, if they really happened to fall out it could be days before they decided to break the silence. In One:Six or Six:One adult/child relationships there won't be much cause for concern unless the One in either case becomes too tyrannical and tries to force his/her opinions on Number Six.

One:Seven

From a professional point of view this combination doesn't have that much going for it. You could probably achieve something together but nothing that could really be looked upon as a great success, and that's what a One looks for in his business life.

The main trouble is that you're both such strong characters who, unfortunately in this instance, express yourselves in entirely different ways — One is a doer who wants to surge ahead and Seven is a thinker who needs to spend much of his or her time alone. Unless you are prepared to make allowances for each other's needs such a partnership would rarely rise to great heights.

One will need to use all his powers of leadershp and, at times, he will need to be downright bossy to keep his partner's feet firmly on the ground and going in the right direction. He'll have to keep his sights set firmly on the target too because Seven has probably forgotten what it is, and he'll have to make sure that his workmate doesn't decide to go off in search of his inner self, leaving him to do everything single-handed.

One could manage very well on his own but in a partnership everyone has to do his fair share of the work. And he must try not to be churlish when Seven comes up with much better ideas than his own — after all Seven spends enough time dreaming them up.

Seven, on the other hand, should try to be more realistic in his approach. Deep spiritual thoughts are all very well in their place but they won't pay the bills. He should also realize that he can't decide to pack his bags and go off on some personal voyage of discovery without telling anyone. He has a job to do and certain responsibilities that he must honour. And his personal philosophies and views on religion are best kept to himself — after all he's the only one who really understands them.

A One working for a Seven Company is a most unlikely combination and One is unlikely to find this relationship rewarding no matter how hard he tries.

The prospect of a Seven working for a One Company looks marginally better because he does have some exceedingly good ideas although he never really knows quite what to do with them.

Within a family One and Seven children would probably only ever meet at meal-times as One would be out seeking adventure and Seven would be locked away in his or her bedroom reading, studying or quietly thinking about something deeply significant. From a parent/child point of view these two will never, ever understand each other. The One adult will despair of the Seven's unworldliness and lack of ambition while the One child will probably decide to leave home as soon as possible in search of fame and fortune.

One:Eight

A One:Eight combination can be either highly successful or absolutely disastrous — there are no shades of grey in between. Unless you're both prepared to make a concerted team effort and keep the more forceful side of your natures under strict control, you might as well call it a day right now. However, if you do accept the challenge that this combination offers, you possess all the ingredients necessary for success, which are courage, determination and the will to succeed.

When we compare your positive qualities we find that Ones and Eights are not dissimilar. You are both strong, practical and imaginative, you certainly know how to cope in an emergency, and you are both intelligent and aggressively ambitious.

However, Ones don't like being told what to do. They are also stubborn and impatient while Eights are unscrupulous, mercenary and pushy. The missing factor, and perhaps the saving grace in this volatile partnership, is self-control which must be added at all times.

Whether we consider a One working for an Eight Company or an

Eight employed by a One the outlook is always the same — great potential for all concerned, ample room for expansion and the promise of ultimate success provided that everybody watches their Ps and Qs and no one steps out of line. If, however, problems do arise they are liable to snowball and the whole situation could rapidly deteriorate with the result that the employers and employees soon part company.

Any family that has One and Eight children within its walls is in for a bumpy ride. When they are being good they're very good and when they are not — watch out!

With the onset of adolescence a One parent is liable to experience trouble with an Eight child. Eights can be sarcastic, defiant and stubborn and a One won't stand that sort of behaviour from anyone. Neither will an Eight parent want his authority challenged, or his plans thwarted by a juvenile One who's just beginning to feel his feet. Stormy is the only word which adequately describes the prevailing conditions within a One:Eight household.

One:Nine

There can be little doubt that this particular partnership will prosper on any level because together you seem to possess a touch of genius. Nine's integrity tempers One's creative flair while his wisdom acts as a sounding-board for the other's often brilliant ideas.

A One:Nine team is virtually unstoppable. Ones are vital and energetic. They always see a project through to the end, need little encouragement and carry their responsibilities unflinchingly.

Nines are visionary, intuitive and highly perceptive. They have quick minds and big ideas although their methods are often slightly unorthodox. They are charming, attractive and inclined to have rather inflated opinions of themselves.

Ones and Nines also have much in common. They're both determined, enterprising and ambitious, have qualities of leadership and individuality. On the debit side they are also impulsive, obstinate and domineering but because Nines possess a far greater depth of understanding they are the only people capable of dismissing a One's aggressive outbursts with little more than an avuncular shrug of the shoulders.

A One seeking employment with a Nine Company would be welcomed with open arms. This is one organization which would be prepared to overlook his bad points because they are far sighted enough to recognize his full potential. Within such a firm his chances of success would be virtually assured although he would have to prove his worth first.

A Nine employed by a One Company should rise quickly from obscurity to a position of power and authority. Nines are positive, inspiring and popular; the sort of people who stand out in a crowd. Ones, in particular, are sufficiently astute to recognize and reward potential so once Nines have been singled out for promotion they rarely look back.

The family circle could only be enhanced by the inclusion of a One and a Nine provided they've established an unwritten code of conduct which they're both prepared to abide by. In any case, a One always knows when he's met his match and a Nine secretly knows that he is sharp enough to maintain the balance of power without too much exertion. Even within a One:Nine parent/child relationship, the respect that has grown up between them over the years is usually sufficient to keep arguments to a minimum.

Two:Two

A pair of Twos make an extremely compatible combination because they automatically understand each other. But they will have to make some major adjustments to their joint outlook if they decide to go into business. The main stumbling block lies in the fact that they're *too* alike for their own good and this could stand in the way of their progress. They will need to be more decisive and know when to act if they hope to get anywhere other than into each other's good books.

What a Two:Two partnership needs to succeed and what it is capable of are two entirely different matters. Twos are sensitive and self-conscious, quiet, tactful and unobtrusive. It goes against their very natures to make a fuss, they lack the confidence to sell their ideas and are terrified of responsibility. What's more, they are forever changing their minds, become depressed when they make a mistake and seem incapable of reaching a decision.

Although they leave a lot to be desired as far as business acumen is concerned, they do have some good points. They are adaptable but will never make the first move, always ready to compromise and once they get over their initial shyness they can be extremely good company.

A Two employed by a Two Company would be a mistake for all concerned. Mr Two hasn't much to offer in terms of ideas or qualifications and because he lacks ambition he certainly wouldn't want to take charge of anything more exciting than the petty cash book. In any case the Two Company would, in all probability, be rather a changeable organization which was up one minute and down the next and because he likes to work in a calm, peaceful environment Mr Two could find the prevailing atmosphere within such a company rather unsettling and hard on his nerves.

A couple of Two children playing happily together are a joy to behold. They are considerate, quite prepared to take turns and never argumentative. They rarely do anything to cause concern and seem to have a great many friends. However, they are easily led and could get into mischief if someone else puts them up to it. The main drawback with any Two is their sensitivity and at times when they feel the world has been less than kind to them they become withdrawn and almost impossible to reach.

Twos make kind, devoted parents and provide the security that a Two child needs. In fact Twos of all ages hate to feel threatened or in any way insecure. Children who are Twos, however, may find themselves wishing for a stronger hand to guide them as they mature. But they would never be so cruel as to voice this opinion to their much loved Two parent.

Two:Three

'How to make friends and influence people' aptly describes this combination because that's what a Two:Three partnership is all about. A Two makes friends easily and a Three can readily turn this to their mutual advantage. This is a promising double act which could work well at any level because the Two is always ready to play second fiddle to his brilliantly daring Three partner.

If we take an overall look at this pair it's not difficult to see how well they are suited. Threes are ambitious; they know exactly where they are going and what they want from life which is fine for a Two as he really hasn't got a clue himself. Threes like to be in command and to tell others what to do. Again this suits a Two because he needs a strong person to guide him and would never dream of questioning authority. Threes also tend to be lucky and Two needs all the luck he can get.

A Three has much to offer; he is versatile, talented, shrewd and creative. He is also loyal, trustworthy, generous and caring. In fact he's the best possible thing that could happen to a Two provided his direct manner of speech doesn't hurt Two's feelings.

Two is a neutral number. His success or failure depends largely on the influences that surround him and they look exceptionally promising with a Three partner to guide his steps. Twos are not born leaders, most of them prefer a secondary role although they're receptive to new ideas and can adapt to changing circumstances provided that their security isn't threatened in the process. What they can, and do, provide in this combination is a reliable back-up to Three's efforts.

Twos would rather be loved and respected than successful and within a Three Company they would be well thought of. This sort of organization could provide just the right kind of background in which a Two could feel at home.

A Three would be quite a catch for a Two Company who needed someone bold and imaginative to fill a key position — a Three would never apply for anything less. They could back his judgement, make good use of his talents and suitably reward his efforts. No one knows how to say 'thank you' better than a Two. And as collateral he could offer his shrewd brain, the innate authority he undoubtedly commands, his unswerving loyalty and perhaps some of his luck.

Within a family Two and Threes complement each other very well although it's always the Three who leads and the Two who tags along just in case he can be useful. Where children are concerned, it's usually the Two who gets left with all the clearing up to do or who gets caught when they have both been up to mischief. A Three:Two parent/child relationship is perhaps easier than a Two:Three because the Three child soon becomes more than a match for the adult and will need to be dealt with firmly if he's not to become precocious or out-of-hand.

Two:Four

The keyword for this combination is 'harmony'. A joint Two:Four business venture could prosper, although perhaps only slowly at first, because a Four knows only too well how to build things up and a Two instinctively provides the oil needed to keep the wheels turning smoothly. They complement each other very well and the possibility of disagreements looks remote.

Twos are conscientious, willing workers who plod along quite happily provided that someone else decides the direction in which they go. They're even tempered, sweet-natured and cheerful although some people may find their indecisiveness and lack of confidence rather irritating. They also tend to get depressed when things go wrong and are inclined to worry unnecessarily over trifling little details. However, when harnessed to a strong partner they are capable of getting through a tremendous workload if it doesn't entail too much responsibility.

In numerology Four is the number of the builder and those whose birthdate reduces to a Four are solid, reliable and dependable. Many achieve success in their own particular field of endeavour and you can be sure that they have worked hard to reach their goal. There are no short cuts for these men and women — everything they accomplish has to be earned. Fours are practical, steady and respectable. They never take risks and like to lay solid foundations before they can even consider the possibility of expansion. They represent security and that's the magnet that will attract a Two every time.

When we consider the possibilities of employment the outlook is much the same whether it's a Two wanting to join a Four company or a Four after a vacancy with a Two — the opportunity for advancement is there although it could be a slow progress. A Four company would undoubtedly offer security. Twos and Fours are both reliable workers and neither of them are impulsive or inclined to take risks so 'slow but sure' is the appropriate phrase for all the interested parties.

Twos and Fours at home rarely fall out over anything, because they all feel safe and secure. Whether it's child/child or parent/child there's nothing which is likely to upset or disturb the balance, even when the children grow up and begin to develop distinct personalities of their own. The final description of this Two:Four analysis must be 'happy families'.

Two:Five

The business outlook appears far from promising for a Two:Five team. A great deal of effort will be required from both parties to get it off the ground let alone keep it afloat.

We all know that Fives can survive very well on their own but here they will need to tone down their natural inclination to go solo. Twos, on the other hand, like a quiet life and because they prefer to stay in the background could well find that unless they make more noise than usual they'll become totally overlooked.

In this combination, a Two will need to pull his or her socks up because his partner is a restless sort of person who is liable to take himself off somewhere at the very moment when he's urgently needed to make a decision or cope with a crisis. He will also need to grow a much thicker skin to withstand a Five's sarcastic remarks; adopt a different attitude towards impulsive actions, and conserve his energy so that he can do the work of two when Five has exhausted all his resources. In fact he'll need to think more than twice before he enters into a Two:Five alliance.

Five, on the other hand, will need to slow down and learn to work at a much slower pace in order to cope with the burden of responsibility that will inevitably fall squarely upon his shoulders. He'll have to keep his mind on the job, be more considerate and less self-indulgent. He must discipline himself to resist that overwhelming urge to speculate — even when the odds look stacked in his favour. In fact he will first have to ask himself if he really wants to enter into a partnership like this at all.

The prospects of a Two with a Five company look poor. He'll be like a fish out of water in such an organization and will have to change his outlook completely if he is to fit in. He flourishes best in a peaceful atmosphere and a Five Company certainly wouldn't be able to offer him that.

A Five seeking employment with a Two company probably wouldn't get further than a preliminary interview. Undoubtedly, he has plenty of admirable qualities but not those that the company is seeking. He is far too highly strung and unpredictable for them and they would be much too cautious and dull for him.

Any family that has a Two and a Five child within its ranks is liable to have problems unless the Five is kept firmly in place and the Two is encouraged to stand up for himself. Without these simple precautions the precocious Five could make the other's life a misery. A Two parent will need to adopt much the same tactics with a Five offspring whereas a Five parent will have to be patient and show understanding if he doesn't want to have a moody, secretive youngster on his hands.

Two:Six

This is not a dynamic number combination. It lacks the fundamental drive and ambition which a successful business partnership needs. This duo, however, get on extremely well together at a personal level but Twos are much too homeloving and Sixes far too artistic to survive for long in the hard, cruel world of commerce.

Two 'the Sensitive' and Six 'the Peacemaker' are best viewed together because they are very much alike — both passive, both introverted and both rather reserved. Two will rarely reach a decision and Six certainly won't push him. Two is forever changing his mind and Six isn't forceful enough to discipline him, and fights shy of responsibility every time.

Six is inclined to view the world through rose-coloured spectacles. He's not particularly concerned about money, provided he has sufficient to cover his immediate needs. They would both be better off pottering about at home or in their gardens than trying to run a business.

A Two employed by a Six Company would be happy because very little would be demanded of him. The Six Company would make allowances for him if he was feeling down or out of sorts and would be full of encouragement when he did achieve some small measure of success.

Six would also fit in well with a Two Company because he is trustworthy, loyal and unlikely to cause problems with the rest of the staff.

The long-term forecast on the home front, whether Two:Six child/child or Two:Six parent/child relationships is for long sunny periods without the remote possibility of any scattered showers to spoil the outlook.

Two:Seven

A Two and a Seven become very aesthetic when together and business life is far too demanding for this combination unless they decide to open a transcendental meditation centre or set up a commune based on some strange religious concept which the Seven has evolved. They are too peaceful and harmonious for their own good and the occasional injection of some worldly friction is needed to force them both to adopt a more realistic outlook on life.

Twos need to be led and would soon fall willing victims to a Seven's mysterious charms. They are receptive and would eagerly absorb all Seven's theories. These factors may make a Two ecstatically happy but they won't make him any money unless he can somehow adapt the Seven's unusual views and turn them into a marketable commodity.

Sevens are studious, scholastic and philosophical; they have the ability to penetrate the unknown in the hope of solving some of life's unanswered riddles. And if they could only put some of their discoveries down on paper, a Two is the right person to help turn their scribblings into a saleable manuscript.

A Two should find a Seven Company rather an attractive proposition because it would be like nothing he had ever come across before. He could be himself and also put his creative imagination to full use. In his quiet, conscientious way he could make progress although he still wouldn't want to shoulder too many responsibilities.

A Seven really doesn't have much to offer any company because he is much too secretive and insular to work as part of a team, although he probably has more to contribute to a Two Company than any other. He is not bothered about money so he would work for little reward. Academically he is probably over-qualified but he is passionately interested in travel and research. If a Two Company had an opening which included either or both of these, he would be their first candidate for the job.

Twos and Sevens within a family generally get on well together because they share common interests. They are both quiet, creative and imaginative. The Seven finds the occult fascinating and the Two also has leanings in that direction. They may even find that a form of telepathic communication develops between them as people of both numbers are frequently gifted with powers of ESP. Whether Two:Seven children, adults or a mixture of both, they should have little reason to quarrel and every reason to develop a lasting bond.

Two:Eight

Twos and Eights can work just as well as they can live together. This combination seems to attract money probably because they are honest, industrious and, above all, utterly reliable. Ask them to get something done by a certain date and you can be sure they will; they could even get the job done slightly ahead of schedule. These people often become good friends as well as business partners although, at times, Eight does tend to overshadow Two with his dynamic personality.

With a strong, guiding influence a Two can achieve a great deal. His negative attitudes towards responsibility and decisions become less of a problem when he is teamed with an Eight. Almost certainly he'll find himself playing his favourite role of second in command in the Two:Eight partnership. As a backroom boy he could attend to all the routine matters involved with running a business secure in the knowledge that Eight is sitting competently at the helm.

An Eight is an entirely different proposition altogether and undoubtedly just the right sort of person to push an unambitious Two in a successful direction. He has a fine head for business, an innate desire to succeed at whatever he does as well as a tenacious spirit, a strong will and a surplus of creative energy. However, he should always remember that shock tactics won't work with a Two. A kind, gentle approach will produce far better results every time.

A Two is quite likely to find himself a nice safe, secure position of obscurity somewhere within an Eight Company where he could quietly get on with his job and not have to worry about anything more important than when to take his holidays. An Eight Company would, for their part, expect a fair day's work for a fair day's pay and would certainly get that from him because diligence and a desire to please are standard fittings for any Two.

An Eight within a Two Company is likely to do well for himself because he usually has a great deal of practical experience to offer, he knows how to use power wisely, is not afraid of hard work and certainly knows how to handle money to the best advantage. In fact, most firms would be pleased to have him on their payroll. Unfortunately, he may not find a Two Company progressive enough and for this reason his chances of commanding a high salary would be proportionately less than within a more go-ahead organization. He may well decide against a Two:Eight employer/employee combination.

Two and Eight children usually agree about most things although it's nearly always the Eight who has all the ideas which the Two seems happy enough to go along with. Eight is the one who needs a parental eye kept on him just in case his ambitious schemes swallow up Two's pocket money as well as his own. He is also a dominant character so every attempt should be made to ensure that his achievements don't eclipse those of his Two brother or sister.

A Two parent could find an Eight child argumentative and a challenge to his authority. A situation like this will need careful handling by the parent to ensure that their relationship as individuals, and within the family unit, doesn't suffer. An Eight parent on the other hand should prove to be more than a match for a growing Two child.

Two:Nine

A Two:Nine partnership, from a business point of view, could turn out to be a real winner. They have much to offer and, when working together for a common cause, they really can't fail. The Two has understanding and reliability to contribute to the partnership which both go well with the imagination, vision and insight of Nine.

A Two may not be dynamic and decisive but his even temper, patience and willingness to co-operate and, when necessary, compromise speak for themselves. Even his changeability and periods of depression rarely manage to detract from his usually good nature.

Nines always manage to give the impression that they've seen it all before because they know exactly what to do and how best to do it. In fact they seem wise beyond their years. They are determined, active and courageous without appearing to be pushy or aggresssive. They have quick minds, high ideals and great imaginations. However their impulsive streak can sometimes lead them into trouble. But with a Two who's willing to do all the donkey work and a Nine who's prepared to fight all the way for what he wants, this team is difficult to fault.

When it comes to a Two with a Nine Company or a Nine with a Two organization the picture remains the same. Whichever way round you choose to look at it Nines have a great deal to offer which can be of direct benefit to a Two whether as potential employers or aspiring employees. A Two:Nine combination is always a good bet.

The same holds true on the home front. Two:Nine children are compatible, as are Two:Nine children/parents. The name of the game here is 'Follow My Leader' and that way everyone comes out on top.

Three:Three

A Three:Three business 'ad-venture' would be rather like driving a car with faulty steering and no brakes — there's no telling where it would end up. Threes are reckless, headstrong people who trust too much to luck. This is a combination of incurable gamblers and the odds on survival together are not stacked in your favour.

But don't go thinking that Threes are worthless just because a Three:Three business partnership looks set for disaster. They do have some very good points which they should develop. Threes are very ambitious, versatile and they think at such high speed that few people can keep up with them. If they would settle down, set their sights on a realistic objective and stop running rings around people it would be a step in the right direction. However, Fortune seems to smile on them and their apparent misfortunes have a way of turning out as blessings in disguise.

A Three working for a Three Company is fraught with problems. Threes are too restless to make good employees — they don't like being told what to do, they fly off the handle at the slightest provocation and their manner of speech is often far too direct. All in all this Three:Three combination doesn't auger well.

Three children should, however, get on like a house on fire; always into mischief, always trying to outdo each other but much too full of the joy of living to fall out for long. A Three:Three parent/child relationship would be much the same with the child always managing to do something amusing when his parent is starting to get a little tetchy.

Three:Four

This combination of numbers demands compromise from both parties.

The Three, who is by nature impulsive, must make allowances for Four's innate caution. And Four, who is always far too busy, must make time to listen to Three's ideas. If these personality differences can be overcome during the early stages, a stable business relationship could then result.

Threes possess a touch of brilliance; they are highly talented and express themselves boldly. They are creative, intelligent, full of original ideas and generally one step ahead of everyone else. However, if they want to get anywhere in combination with a Four, they will have to stop being so frivolous, take life a little more seriously, learn to be less extravagant and not lay down the law all the time — a Four must be allowed to have his say too.

Fours are solid, practical people who make excellent administrators and handle money wisely. They are industrious, methodical, hard-working and utterly trustworthy. They're also rather unadventurous which a Three might find a bit dull. They never do anything on the spur of the moment because it seems like a good idea. Everything has to be planned and budgeted for and until that's done they won't make a move. Security is everything to a Four and his natural caution could be the cause of a few arguments in partnership with a Three.

A Four Company would probably be delighted to employ Threes because they are undoubtedly very clever people but it would certainly have to keep a very close watch on them. A Three on the other hand dislikes being in a subordinate position and he could find constant surveillance rather more than he's prepared to take from any employer.

A Four would definitely be an asset to a Three Company because reliable, efficient and well-organized staff are hard to come by. Unfortunately a Four may not have such a high regard for his Three employer, who uses corner-cutting methods which are not to his taste.

Within a family Three and Four children probably won't get on at all. Threes are bold and daring, Fours are cautious and unadventurous — there's simply no common ground for them to play on. In a Three:Four adult/child relationship a Three parent would probably wonder how he ever managed to produce such a conservative child while the child in question would be wishing his parent would take him more seriously. A Four:Three adult/child combination would be just as frustrating for both parties with the adult wishing that his bright, lively youngster would stop being so scatter-brained and make better use of his talents. And the child would resent his parent's attempts to calm him down and to organize his life. A Three child can't help it if he gets bored easily, he needs to express himself in his own way and try everything at least once.

Three:Five

These two numbers, when combined, produce many viable ideas which the Five knows exactly how to market once the Three has 'packaged' them attractively. They are bound to succeed. The only danger in this partnership lies in haste. Threes and Fives are both inclined to act impulsively on occasion.

Threes have the luck of the devil. They are creative, artistic individuals with a bold, imaginative style all of their own. They also have shrewd minds, the ability to concentrate on more than one thing at a time and a strong sense of order and justice. From a negative point of view, they can also be domineering, critical and pessimistic.

Fives are lovable rogues. They would probably have been pirates or outlaws two hundred years ago but now they're just restless soldiers of fortune who live on their nerves and crave nothing more from life than a little excitement every now and then. They are impatient and highly-strung, born speculators, always more than ready to run the odd risk, and, above all, resilient. They have the enviable ability to recover quickly from any misfortune.

A Three:Five/Five:Three employer/employee combination could go either way. There's such a powerful mixture of ingredients here that the end result could either turn out to be a resounding success coupled with substantial financial rewards or an utter disaster.

Three and Five children within the same family would be a handful and any parent faced with such a problem combination would need the patience of a saint as well as eyes in the back of their head to keep control. These children would be happy enough together but the mischief they could get up to doesn't bear thinking about.

A Three:Five parent/child relationship would be marginally better as the enlightened Three would probably do everything to encourage the growing Five to enjoy his independence and do his own thing. And a Five parent is the last person to criticize anyone with a zest for life least of all his own child.

Three:Six

These two ought to do well together because they have similar personalities and outlooks. If they decide to go into partnership they should be able to overcome most obstacles in their way. The rewards could be enormous. In the world of business, people with this combination of numbers often form partnerships for life.

They are both creative and artistic individuals — Sixes in particular are good with colour and many have perfect colour vision. They both respect and admire intelligence in others and neither suffers fools gladly. Loyalty is another characteristic they share along with friendly natures, magnetic personalities and interesting conversation.

Now the bad news — Threes can be critical, domineering and dictatorial while Sixes are inclined to be selfish, domineering and self-opinionated. They can't possibly get their own way all the time and, on analysis, this looks like the main problem area.

A Three could make progress with a Six Company as long as he's prepared to take his work seriously and provided he doesn't decide to engage the managing director in a battle of wits — he could easily win the debate but his future wouldn't look too rosy after that. He would also need to accept the discipline and limitations that working for someone else would naturally impose. Sixes respect intelligence, so from the company's point of view, they would be prepared to give him a chance.

A Six could work in harmony for a Three Company because the vibrations for these two numbers are in tune on a business level. A Six is open-minded, well-balanced and self-controlled while a Three company is go-ahead, original and lively. Together they could strike the right chord and perhaps even try a few close harmonies at some later stage.

At home children whose birthdate reduce to Three or Six should have plenty in common. They are both intelligent, talented children who could produce some startling results if allowed to give full vent to their artistic skills. But, because they like to get their own way, the occasional tantrum is only to be expected.

When Three:Six parents and children are combined the Three adult is usually sufficiently versatile to adapt to his child's changing needs and emotions. And because a Six likes to be in a happy environment, especially at home, he'll be only too ready to restore the peace whenever necessary.

Sixes make conscientious, dedicated parents and a Three child should be able to develop into a happy, well-balanced adult with such a parent as his guide and mentor.

Three:Seven

Three and Seven make a very complementary couple at any level and if they always remember to give each other sufficient room to breathe they won't go far wrong.

Threes are full to the brim with brilliant ideas. They're original, daring, imaginative and versatile. They like to be able to express themselves boldly in their work through the use of their creative talents. They are also singularly proud, dislike feeling under an obligation to anyone and are rather inclined to speak their minds at times when a discreet silence would be sensible.

Sevens are equally strong characters but tend to hide their light under a bushel rather more than a Three, who loves attention. They have inquiring minds, penetrating intellects and an overwhelming desire to find at least some of the answers to life's mysteries. They too are creative, artistic and, at times, brilliant although, unlike a Three, Sevens need to spend some time on their own to collect their thoughts. And they too can be just as impulsive and unreasonable as their partners. This Three:Seven liaison has great potential.

In a Three:Seven employee/employer relationship this potential still exists because a Three is shrewd and ambitious — he never misses a trick — and a Seven Company would be understanding enough to realize that, more than anything else, Three needs to channel and develop his creative talents in a useful direction.

A Seven, unfortunately, is a difficult person to place with any company, not because he's a trouble-maker but because few firms have an opening for a secretive, intellectual mystic. Three, however, is the number of enlightenment, so perhaps such a company would see potential in him that others had failed to recognize. He is good at research, loves to travel and is sufficiently wise and knowledgeable to guide others even if he often fails to find the right direction for himself.

On the home front, Three and Seven children probably wouldn't want to spend all their time together but while Three went off to explore with his friends, Seven would probably take the opportunity to catch up on some reading in the peace and quiet of his own room.

Sevens make marginally better parents because they are far more understanding than Threes who tend to apply force rather than persuasion. A Seven child might have a more exciting upbringing with a Three parent (who prefers action rather than words) than a Three child with a Seven parent who prefers the opposite.

Three:Eight

A Three:Eight combination works better at a business level than in a personal relationship. Both are inclined to have big ideas and, when combined, they possess the ability to convert them into reality. Three is the communicator who goes out establishing contacts, taking orders and negotiating deals while Eight has the business brain that controls the whole operation. If they are both aiming for the same goal there is little that can really stop them.

Again this is another partnership best viewed as a whole because the abilities of both partners tend to overlap and the talents of one frequently become enhanced by some ability the other possesses. Threes want to be successful and with a strong, practical Eight to guide them there's no reason why they shouldn't. Eight is a tough, hard, businessman who needs someone energetic, charming and persuasive to do all the running about while he takes executive charge of the business. He's tenacious, obstinate and ruthless — in fact the very person to ensure Three toes the line and takes his responsibilities seriously. Like Eights, Threes are shrewd and observant, they are also highly talented, full of original ideas, extremey versatile and incredibly lucky. This combination can't go wrong even if they argue about things because arguments are something they both rather enjoy and they are both evenly matched on that score.

The Three:Eight employee/employer and Eight:Three employee/employer combinations present much the same picture as a partnership, because there are benefits for all.

These favourable trends even follow on into the home with each number ultimately benefitting, and somehow managing to enhance, the other. Three:Eight children are bold and energetic. A certain amount of rivalry is only to be expected but as they grow older they should be able to help each other out in many ways. Although a Three parent may be a little too frivolous to appreciate fully the potential of his ambitious Eight child, he can help in many aspects of the child's development. On the other hand, in the guise of parent, a powerful Eight should have plenty of useful contacts when it comes to finding his talented Three son or daughter a good school or a suitable career opening.

Three:Nine

This is an extremely compatible combination, provided neither of you has to work for a living. However, as most of us have to earn our livings the message for a Three:Nine partnership is to become more realistic, down to earth and practical if you want to get anywhere in life, especially if you ever hope to make any money.

Three has a lot to learn. For a start he should realize that wit and charm alone are not enough to guarantee him a living. He should be less bold and more diligent, less wasteful and generally take work a little more seriously. His main problem is that he can do many things passably, but none particularly well. He needs to specialize if he doesn't want to become just a Jack-of-all-trades.

Nines can be too high-minded and visionary for their own good. And they tend towards egotism, intolerance, petty-mindedness and prejudice. Both partners in this combination will have their work cut out to pull themselves together and get into a businesslike frame of mind before they can even consider taking this Three:Nine venture any further.

In a Three:Nine employee/company combination a Three could do moderately well for himself because Nine can be quite a strong number, provided that the impulsiveness and high ideals associated with it are kept in perspective and not allowed to interfere with progress. Three, however, could find a Nine organization rather dull after a time and his chances of promotion wouldn't be so great as with perhaps a One or an Eight Company.

Strangely enough, a positive, clear-thinking Nine could be just what a Three company needs to temper some of its more outrageous ideas. Three is a bold, lively number and because Nine sees most things on a very broad scale his opinions and criticisms could be of tremendous value. But he could find such a company too insensitive to the needs of others and not sufficiently concerned about the environment to remain interested in their schemes for long.

On the home front, well away from the pressures and problems of business life, Threes and Nines coexist in perfect harmony. Children of these numbers find no trouble in amusing themselves and the Three:Nine/Nine:Three adult/child combinations rarely have cause to complain about each other. People of both numbers are impulsive, a little unorthodox and rather inclined to make the odd foolish mistake but because Three is adaptable and Nine broadminded, they rarely give each other cause for worry.

Four:Four

A partnership such as this can sometimes seem to epitomize those 'Jones's' we often try to 'keep up with'. They are compatible, financially successful, materially secure and lucky into the bargain. Any business they enter into will quite naturally expand, bu they will have to watch out because they risk becoming so materially minded that other aspects of life just pass them by. All work and no play could make these 'builders' dull boys and girls.

Fours are paragons of virtue. They are practical, steady, calm, respectable, efficient and industrious. They're extremely well organized and very down to earth. They are good at handling money, utterly trustworthy and certainly not afraid of hard work. But they have an inborn need to feel secure and for this reason they never take hasty or spontaneous action. They are also inclined to brood a great deal and worry over problems that exist only in their own minds. Even so, prospects for this Four:Four partnership can only be described as 'golden'.

There's nothing much more to add when it comes to a Four:Four employer/employee combination. A Four Company wants to build itself into an empire and who better to help it do just that than another like-minded Four? A Four company offers stability and permanence, and a Four employee is almost prepared to sell his soul to secure a safe, steady job with good prospects.

In the security of their own homes Fours may not be surrounded by art, literature and music but they are sure to have plenty of status symbols prominently displayed as testaments to their money-making prowess. Four children usually play happily with simple building bricks at first and then they progress on to sophisticated construction kits with countless accessories to add to their enjoyment. Four parents never seem to lose their childhood fascination for such things either. Unadventurous and down to earth they may be but Fours of any age always get along well together.

Four:Five

Opposites often attract and this is just the case here. With a concerted effort on both sides this working combination can achieve success. Fours are solid and Fives are imaginative; Fours are practical and Fives are adjustable; once these opposites gain balance they can work to each other's favour.

Four would undoubtedly be the steadying influence in this partnership. They have plenty of commonsense and a Five needs someone like this to keep him in order. They are calm, unflappable, practical and hardworking, good with money, well organized, efficient and tenacious. In fact they are quite the opposite of a Five who needs someone to sort him out and handle finances.

Fives find it hard to settle; they like to be on the go all the time, burning off some of their nervous energy. They are incurable gamblers, impatient, impulsive and highly strung. They seem to crave excitement and many live on their nerves until the strain becomes too great and they come quickly down to earth again. All these aspects of their characters will need to be drastically toned down, if not totally eliminated, to fit in a Four's orderly attitude to life. However, Fives are also highly intelligent, creative, original and perceptive. They are resilient and bounce back quickly from the heaviest blow. With a reliable Four at the helm, at tight rein on Five's spirit of adventure and an optimistic attitude, these two could go far, and achieve a great deal.

In an employee/employer combination the opposites repel as they lack a common denominator like an equal partnership to provide the balance. Four doesn't want to work for a Five organization which lacks stability and the employers are probably looking for someone rather more dynamic than him to fill their key positions. In the same way, Five certainly doesn't want to get involved with a stodgy Four Company who would probably regard him with extreme suspicion if he applied for their dull, mundane vacancy. The prospects on this Four:Five job front are virtually non-existent.

At home it's a slightly different story. Fours and Fives can get along tolerably well if they both decide to make the effort. But without that vital component you would have more success trying to mix oil with water or compare chalk with cheese. They just don't mix without a generous helping of hard work.

Four:Six

A Four and a Six are just the right ingredients for a sound business relationship, and a personal one too. This combination, when it occurs in the business world, is often connected with the leisure industry, entertainment or advertising. Both partners work hard and play hard and this balance of activities is undoubtedly the secret that lies behind their happiness and success.

Fours have a distinct character all of their own and seem to take a perverse delight in viewing everything from the opposite angle to everyone else. They are positive and unconventional in their views and opinions, extremely well-disciplined and practical. They are also efficient, organized and can at times be rather thin-skinned.

Sixes, the other half of this capable double act, are also well balanced, reliable and self-controlled. They're resourceful, creative, conventional and homely. They can be very determined when it comes to carrying out their plans and very obstinate in the face of opposition. And when really impassioned about something, they have been known to force their opinions on those around them.

There are no real flaws in this combination which need to be worked at or improved as both partners know what they want and where they are heading.

Four and Six are two numbers which vibrate in harmony and when it comes to applying for a job both have much to offer that would interest a company of the opposite number. And because they are also two fairly conventional, well-balanced numbers it seems likely that a mutually rewarding Four:Six employee/employer relationship could develop.

Children of these numbers are sure to get along as they're so evenly matched although Four will always be the more practical of the pair and Six the more artistic. People ruled by the numbers Four and Six are peaceful homelovers at heart. Even their adult/child relationships should be reasonably trouble-free and harmonious most of the time, even during adolescence.

Four:Seven

This is a combination of numbers which promises great achievements because it is balanced by the best characteristics of both worlds. Four, the Builder, provides the solid foundations for the often brilliant ideas of Seven, the Mysterious, to stand upon and grow.

Let's look at Four first because he's the linchpin of the whole venture; take away his backing and the Seven would be left without a leg to stand upon. Fours have many talents that will benefit this partnership. They're good at handling money so they can keep the books; they never get into a flap, so they can keep the peace, and they are so efficient and well organized that Seven won't have to concern himself at all with day to day administration. They are hard-working, down to earth, full of common sense and never, ever take risks.

With Four as the strong, unshakeable partner in this combination, and probably the financier too, Seven can afford to be himself and take things at his own pace. Once allowed to do this free from restrictions and heavy responsibilities, his powerful, educated mind can be given free rein and an endless stream of clever ideas should begin to flow. This is where Four steps in again to convert them into viable, marketable, well-packaged realities. He couldn't get on so well without his brainy partner any more than Seven could make such progress without Four, but together they are quite a team.

A Four should never be out of work for long as his skills are always in great demand but he is much too down to earth and set in his ways to be seriously interested in working for a mysterious, intellectual Seven organization although they would undoubtedly jump at the chance to take him onto their payroll.

Sevens, on the other hand, often find themselves at a loose end because they don't have a realistic attitude towards their careers. It's hard to realize that behind those dreamy expressions lurk brilliant minds. There's no reason to suppose they would be particularly attractive to a Four Company but there again they just might be useful somewhere within such an organization if only they would smarten themselves up and becomes more business-like.

The mood is one of neutrality when Fours and Sevens are found together within a family. Fours, whether adults or children, tend to get on with the day to day routine of living without ever giving a second thought to the deep, profound meaning behind it all. They find it almost impossible to understand what this strange person (Seven) who lives in the same close unit is talking about.

Sevens — adults or children — tend to find the Four members of their family rather dull and too preoccupied with functioning efficiently. Without someone on their own wavelength to communicate with they tend to withdraw even further into themselves. This Four:Seven combination rarely provokes arguments because they have so little in common over which to fall out.

Four:Eight

A Four:Eight combination makes a superb business team and the balance they achieve doesn't stop there. This is one partnership which can include friendship on its lists of assets. The reason for their success is quite simple — Eight sees everything on a very large scale while Four tends to see things in greater detail and so he can put minor errors right before they do any great damage to the overall scheme. In fact Eight is rather like a landscape gardener — he comes up with the sweeping plan while Four is in the greenhouse carefully weeding out any damaged or misshapen seedlings that would fail to grow into perfect specimens.

In numerology Four plus Eight can be looked at from the point of view Builder (Four) plus Materialist (Eight) which equals material growth, and safe foundations with a guaranteed return.

Fours are capable organizers with exceptional powers of systemization. They are hard-working, energetic, industrious, steady and reliable. They rarely become flustered and seldom get down-hearted. In short they are the perfect partners for strong, tough, materialistic Eights.

Eights are wise, imaginative and hell-bent on making a success of their lives. They seek money and social position and never fail to take advantage of any opportunity that will help them achieve their aims. They are responsible, self-disciplined, adaptable and tenacious. At times, they can be downright unscrupulous as well as hard and selfish. Nothing can really stop a combination like this.

The partnership prospects carry through onto the job front. A Four Company would be extremely foolish to turn down an Eight's application for employment and once safely ensconced in such an organization he should go from strength to strength until he reaches the top. A Four may not quite reach the top of an Eight Company but he should come pretty close — he would be more likely to finish up in control of his own department rather than running the whole organization. Remember, Eight is a number with big ideas and Fours view everything on a much smaller scale.

When a combination of Four and Eight children occurs in a family, Eight will automatically be the boss with Four as second-in-command. This arrangement works very well and few problems should arise — unless they demand a whole years' pocket money in advance, with collateral of course, to finance some scheme of theirs! It could even be worth consideration. The parent/child combinations paint much the same picture of balanced outlooks, responsible attitudes and few major worries.

Four:Nine

A Four and a Nine have much to teach each other but as the learning process is always rather slow this combination works better in private than during business hours. Nines are wise and can impart much valuable knowledge to a Four who, in turn, can pass on many practical skills that Nine would otherwise not acquire.

Four realizes that you will never achieve anything if you don't work hard but his concept of success is poles apart from that of a Nine. He sees it as having ample security, a comfortable home, a good steady job and being able to afford a car, an annual holiday and the odd evening out, whereas a Nine sees success more as a state of mind. Nines would feel they had achieved something only when they were in a position to show others the right way to live through their own breadth of thinking.

It's very easy to see how both partners can benefit from an exchange of ideas but almost impossible to visualize how a Four:Nine partnership will ever prosper.

However, the outlook for this combination of numbers in employment looks marginally better. Four is a steady, reliable worker and a Nine company, probably with worldwide interests, would be looking for solid, practical men and women to see that they are efficiently managed. Unfortunately, Four is a homelover so he may not be prepared to work away from his family for any great length of time.

Nines have an intense urge to serve in a cause so if a Four Company happened to be involved in a charitable or humanitarian line of business he could be their man. But if they were manufacturers of sanitary fittings, estate agents or offering truck rentals, neither would be of interest to the other.

In the home people of both numbers will need to make allowances within this Four:Nine combination. The Four child will have to realize that his brother/sister doesn't find bricks quite such fascinating playthings as he does and the Nine child will have to be more patient when others don't share his high ideals. Four parents are practical so a Nine child can expect to be guided in a useful direction. A Four child's attempts to organize everything will be suffered in silence by his wise Nine parents.

Five:Five

This is an extremely dangerous combination from whichever angle you choose to view it — business partners, employee/employer, child/child or parent/child. Fives are restless, changeable, highly exciteable and liable to rebel against any form of restraint. Put two Fives together and this creates a potentially explosive partnership which should be avoided if possible.

Five:Six

When a temperamental, excitable Five is coupled with a quiet, peaceloving Six he undergoes a very marked change of personality. The calming influence of a Six enables him to put his thoughts in better order and the resulting partnership could prove stimulating for both.

Fives are like icebergs; seven-eighths of them lies hidden beneath the water. If they would only calm down for five minutes and allow you to take a proper look at them you would be surprised at what is lying hidden there below the surface. Fives are clever, resilient and resourceful despite their restless natures. They can also be creative, original, perceptive and extremely fine judges of character and worth. They do many things well, make friends easily and recover quickly from misfortunes. All they need is a Six to pacify them a little so that their hidden potential can be brought forward and developed.

Sixes can calm anything from a storm in a teacup to a violent tempest of emotions so it should be a relatively simple task for them to steer a Five onto a more even course. Sixes are well-balanced, open-minded and self-controlled. And Five needn't think he can ride rough-shod over a Six — once determined to get him working properly Six can be very obstinate and unyielding. However, Sixes probably won't have to resort to a show of force because they intuitively understand the needs and difficulties of others, and seem to get the best from them by employing a system of rewards. This Five:Six combination may not make the front page of *The Financial Times* but it shouldn't appear in the bankruptcy column either.

On the job scene, a Five working for a Six Company should be reasonably well-placed if his job included travel or communications. A Six working for a changeable Five Company would quickly find himself involved in personnel management because they would need somebody calm and diplomatic to quieten down the workforce after they had decided to make even more sweeping changes. Not golden prospects for either number, but prospects nonetheless.

At home, where Six is usually in his element, there could be some problems with this combination not perhaps where Five:Six children are concerned (they should muddle along with nothing more than the odd fight or argument) but probably in the adult/child relationships. Fives crave adventure, excitement and travel. They want to leave home as soon as possible to see the world and a Six parent could find his child's determination to leave upsetting. Sixes need peaceful, stable homes and children of this number could be faced with the reverse situation — a Five parent who wants to keep moving house, changing area and sometimes even wanting to emigrate.

Five:Seven

This combination of numbers seldom works for long as the exciteable Five invariably becomes too much for the retiring Seven to cope with. Sevens need peace and quiet in order to be able to hear themselves think and a Five is the least likely of all the numbers to furnish them with that.

Even if Five takes a solemn oath not to make a noise, not to change his mind and never to speculate, he's so jumpy and highly strung that his mere presence would be more than enough to irritate a Seven beyond measure and ruin his concentration; how can he possibly be expected to think with this lunatic always in and out, drumming his fingers and forever straightening his tie? And when Five has eventually exhausted all his nervous strength and has finally succumbed to a nervous breakdown, Seven certainly won't want to do all Five's work on top of his own. Any plans for a combination like this probably won't even get past the drawing-board stage before somebody blows a fuse.

Five:Seven and Seven:Five job combinations will probably be rather short-lived affairs too. The individuals involved are not compatible with the overall needs and viewpoint of the respective companies concerned. How can a madcap, adventurous Five ever hope to fit into an intellectual, high-minded organization or, for that matter, a lone Seven into a somewhat unstable, restless environment?

Within a family Fives and Sevens rarely get along either. Seven wants peace and quiet and Five makes far too much noise. Unless someone decides to divide the house into separate halves using the breakfast room as 'no man's land', there's really no solution to the Five:Seven child/child or adult/child' family problems.

Five:Eight

You had better watch out when these two dynamic personalities join forces because an Eight can convert ideas into reality almost as fast as a Five can dream them up. This is a winning business partnership while it lasts but does tend to burn itself out if someone doesn't apply the brakes in time.

Five is a born gambler. He loves to speculate and he certainly wouldn't be able to resist the temptation to put his shirt on a Five:Eight combination because the odds are so very much in its favour. Fives are unpredictable, ungovernable characters but they do come up with some wonderful ideas. They are clever, creative, original and if they can only discipline themselves to take things one step at a time and give their full attention to the immediate matter in hand they won't go far wrong. They are perceptive, selective, astute and have a positive genius for organizing other people which, unfortunately, doesn't seem to extend as far as themselves. More application and less impulsiveness would be the making of them.

Eight is the number of worldly success and people whose birthdates reduce to it are tough, materialistic and practical. They make excellent businessmen because they can be hard, aggressive and even thoroughly unscrupulous in some circumstances as well as being cautious, persuasive and diplomatic in others. They are responsible, adaptable, tireless, wise and sometimes positively crafty.

Fives ought to go far within an Eight Company although 'far' in this instance doesn't necessarily indicate travel which they love. Perhaps 'up' would have been a better choice of word because their bright ideas, adaptability and talent for wise delegation should quickly take them to a high position in such an enterprise. Eights recognize potential when it's staring them in the face and an Eight Company certainly wouldn't let a clever, if rather restless, fellow like Five slip through their net.

An Eight could easily take charge of any company because he's a person with 'top management' written all over him. He is poised, self-assured, determined and can usually boast a great deal of practical experience. A Five company would be suitable for him because they wouldn't be afraid to take the odd calculated risk or try their hand at something a little unorthodox or adventurous.

On the home front Five and Eight children will probably play peacefully one moment and be at each other's throats the next. Unfortunately it's just the way they are but the periods of truce should gradually lengthen as they grow older and learn more self-control. Five children always benefit from the guidance of an Eight parent but from the parent's point of view they could secretly wish that their child would make better use of his talents and that he wouldn't lose interest just when he's starting to show promise in a particular field. Eight children are rather inclined to get a little too big for their boots during adolescence but Fives can usually hold their own in a battle of wits and seldom bear a grudge. In fact they will probably seem more like friends to their children than the traditional figure of authority that a parent so often tends to represent.

Five:Nine

When it occurs this Five:Nine combination can be moderately successful because Five knows exactly how Nine should pass on his knowledge and wisdom in the most profitable way. This partnership cuts both ways and Nines seem to have the knack of getting the best out of Fives without appearing to move a muscle.

Fives make wonderful dealers and salesmen — they're highly-strung, live on their nerves, are capable of reaching quick decisions and not afraid to take chances. They are clever, sharp, perceptive and resourceful. Life is one long adventure for them; they like to try everything at least once and hate to feel that they are in a rut. However, they are very adaptable so they could go from dealing in antiques or selling insurance one week to second-hand cars and encylopaedias the next.

Nines need someone sharp like a Five to keep an eye on them because for all their high-minded ideals and wide sympathies they really do make some ridiculous mistakes. They tend to speak without thinking and often act impulsively. This is really the main cause of their problems, coupled with the fact that they're usually so preoccupied with trying to make the world a better place to live in, that they don't really notice what's going on around them.

A Five may not find it so easy to get along when actually employed by a Nine Company as he's more concerned about his own survival than anyone else's. Fives don't really want to work for someone else and never settle anywhere for long, so their prospects don't look too good in this Five:Nine employment combination. Nine's fate with a Five Company is equally unpromising. In many ways he's too good for a company like this and is probably too much of a 'do-gooder' to fit into a commercial operation.

In a family setting children of these numbers tend to do their own thing rather than having shared hobbies and interests as many brothers and sisters do, although Five would probably decide to have a go at anything Nine was involved in just for the sheer hell of it.

Five:Nine and Nine:Five parent/child combinations seldom share the same opinions. Fives — whether adult or child — are restless and impatient. They never really manage to understand the visionary, humanitarian point of view of their Nine parent or child.

Six:Six

Sixes are creative, resourceful and imaginative. They have an eye for colour and a positive genius for home and family life. Not the best credentials for a business enterprise but they can be singularly determined when it comes to carrying out their plans. They are exceptionally self-reliant and particularly adept at handling difficult people. Add to this the fact thay they're well-balanced, self-controlled, and good mediators and they could get somewhere with a Six:Six partnership. But there's always one important proviso with Sixes — somewhere along the line there must be sufficient scope for them to use their innate artistic and creative talents. Denying them this right is like trying to run a car without petrol — they won't move an inch in any direction.

A Six employed by a Six Company may not be a particularly rewarding liaison in terms of money but it will be as far as job satisfaction is concerned. This organization could provide the peaceful atmosphere that Six thrives in and they'd automatically have plenty of outlets for his particular talents.

In the home they should all live happily surrounded by beautiful ornaments, rich colour, sculpture and music. Sixes also have a great passion for books and if they can't boast a library they're sure to have plenty of bookshelves about the place all groaning under the weight of their contents. It's roses all the way for any combination of Sixes in their halcyon, happy homes.

Six:Seven

This combination is a non-starter and should be immediately scratched from the list of runners. Common ground, which is vital for business communications is non-existent in a Six:Seven relationship and is likely to be the cause of any failures.

Sevens spend so much time alone that they never really appreciate or indeed even notice what a Six has been doing. Similarly, Sixes tend to spend all their time being creative and they never bother to find out what a Seven has been doing.

Only superhuman efforts could save this combination whether it's in a business partnership, or employee/employer, child/child or parent/child relationships.

Six:Eight

This combination has great potential because the roles of each partner are clearly defined. An Eight knows how to assume control and decide the best direction to take while a Six is perfectly happy to give support, offer ideas and generally provide the window-dressing.

You can depend on Sixes for many reasons. They are equable, conventional, well-balanced and utterly trustworthy. They are also just, kind, understanding and have great moral courage. They can be seen at their best when involved in some kind of creative activity where their artistic talents, superb imaginations and eye for colour can be fully extended.

Eights are strong, practical and wise. They represent money, power and success. They have tremendous reserves of energy which they can call upon in any emergency and are never afraid to take full responsibility for their actions, which can sometimes be very ruthless. They are self-assured, hard-working, have their own definition for the word 'honesty' and an inbuilt desire to build an empire of their own.

Again the Six:Eight combination looks promising in an employee/employer relationship. This is because the roles are still clearly defined. Both parties will know exactly what is expected and what to expect in return. The prospects of promotion are high because each individual is well suited to his or her tasks.

In the home children whose birthdates reduce to an Eight tend to be rather bossy with their brothers and sisters but a peacemaking Six won't let that bother him for a moment. He knows just how to handle difficult characters and will soon have Eight eating out of his hand and still thinking he's top dog.

A Six parent may need to clamp down rather hard on a bumptious

Eight teenager who is inclined to get on his high horse from time to time. But he'll never find a more loving, dedicated parent than a Six. Eight parents, on the other hand, will rarely feel their authority is being questioned by a Six child.

Six:Nine

This numerical combination is always something special because it combines beauty (six) with truth (nine). Sixes and Nines instinctively know how to give and take at all levels of consciousness. A partnership like this rarely breaks up.

Sixes are loyal, faithful, sympathetic individuals who function best in a calm, peaceful atmosphere. They simply can't cope with forceful, opinionated people and often go to great lengths to avoid them. They are balanced, open-minded, controlled in their actions and often make superb mediators because they can see both sides of any argument or problem without bias. They avoid quarrels, respect intelligence and are quick to respond to the needs of others.

Nine is the number of high mental and spiritual achievement and those ruled by it are large-minded, visionary and idealistic. They need a good cause to espouse, something to crusade about or a twentieth century holy war to fight before they even begin to feel remotely fulfilled. While these attitudes are highly commendable, they won't be much use in a business partnership. Fortunately Nines do have some other qualities which would be useful. They are determined, active, courageous and enterprising. They have clear, quick minds and a good imagination although they tend to fall down when it comes to common sense. This Six:Nine combination certainly doesn't represent a dynamic duo of budding tycoons but with application, effort and a little bit of luck they could do moderately well.

Job prospects look poor and a meteoric rise to fame and fortune for a Six employed by a Nine Company or a Nine employed by a Six organization seems out of the question.

Happily on the home front it's a much better picture altogether. Six:Nine children can play their games of give and take in perfect harmony and the adult/child combination can exchange 'home truths' and 'beautiful' thoughts. And so long as the outside world isn't allowed to come in through the front door too often, everything between them should be plain sailing.

Seven:Seven

When two Sevens get together they make a perfect team. Occasionally they develop a form of mental telepathy and when this occurs all words become superfluous. But they live in a world of their own which is peopled by their thoughts and which, unfortunately, is totally divorced from reality. This combination must develop a more materialistic approach to life, and the sooner the better, if they want to survive. Any thoughts about a business partnership are a waste of time — it just can't work.

Sevens are mysterious, secretive, philosophical, confusing and completely out of touch. They love to travel, although they never seem to do it in comfort, generally neglect their material needs, having absolutely no idea at all about money and prefer their own company to that of others. They're intuitive, over-imaginative, studious and creative. It's for these reasons that a working partnership is unlikely to succeed.

The Seven:Seven employee/employer combination is equally doubtful. But the home environment is one place where Seven:Seven combinations can really flourish. Their relationship is like a marriage of minds or a never-ending quest for truth.

Seven:Eight

Seven and Eight work reasonably well together in a business partnership because somehow the Seven has a calming effect on the Eight and manages not only to keep his restless energy in check but also channelled in a constructive direction. Seven has a strange visionary quality about him which could almost be described as 'second sight' and this is invaluable as far as forward planning is concerned.

There is something very different about a Seven and this is what Eight finds particularly fascinating. How can such a studious, intellectual individual who cares nothing for riches and worldly success manage to exert such an influence over him? — and exert it he certainly does.

Perhaps it's because he doesn't retaliate when Eight gets too aggressive but simply dismisses his outpourings with a philosophical shrug of his shoulders. Or is it the way he can always gauge what Eight's mood will be before he's even spoken to him? These are all questions Eight will probably never manage to answer but the fact remains — Seven can control the situation whenever he chooses.

Eights are charming, dignified and worldly wise. They want to succeed more than anything else in the world. They're strong, adaptable, practical and determined. Eights are often much misunderstood and many feel intensely lonely at heart but they manage to conceal their true feelings very well and allow people to think just what they like. This combination should be able to live up to expectations and produce some positive results.

A Seven:Eight employee/employer relationship doesn't look good because Seven is neither sufficiently practical not determined to cope with the demands this company would undoubtedly make upon him. However, an Eight working for a Seven company, or almost any other organization for that matter, should be able to rise to a position of some authority.

Sevens and Eights when they appear in a family will probably have little in common. Eights are always positive, aggressive characters who know what they want and are prepared to fight for it. Sevens are the opposite. They are quiet, thoughtful people who probably don't want anything more than to be left alone.

Children of these numbers will probably follow their own separate interests rather than play together and the adult/child combinations will never really see eye to eye. Eight parents want their children to be successful, Seven children want to go to university and stay there forever learning and researching in sympathetic surroundings. Seven parents don't know enough about the world to offer the right sort of advice to an Eight child who wants to get on in life.

Seven:Nine

Peace, harmony and perfect understanding are all qualities to be found within a Seven:Nine relationship. their two minds think as one. Unfortunately they're both in real danger of becoming so spiritual in their outlook that they lose touch with reality. A Seven:Nine combination will never make a satisfactory business partnership unless it's involved with the organization of humanitarian projects.

Sevens are independent, original and strongly attracted to all things magical or mysterious. They like to travel, although seldom in comfort and never along well-beaten tourist tracks, in order to gain first-hand knowledge of people and other cultures. They have powerful minds, penetrating intellects, wonderful imaginations and a dreamy side to their characters. When combined with Nines, they often become concerned about political issues.

All Nines care passionately about the problems of providing famine relief to Third World countries, they are worried about the nuclear arms race, they have high ideals and a genuine love of humanity. They are sincere, but on occasions misguided, do-gooders. Teamed with a Seven they will never set the business world on fire but they may just be able to do something, however small, to improve conditions in the outside world.

As far as the Seven:Nine job combinations are concerned, there is little on offer. Seven and Nine Companies both need men and women with business acumen to keep them running efficiently, not thoughtful, solitary mystics or people who are so concerned about everyone else that their minds are not on the job.

Who said that you couldn't put wise heads on young shoulders? Seven and Nine both have them. And there's always a distinct feeling of 'live and let live' or maybe even 'each to his own' in a Seven:Nine household.

Eight:Eight

When two Eights decide to co-operate the result is likely to be a well-run, dynamic team which is completely geared for success. There are no shades of grey for this combination, it's one of those 'all or nothing' relationships which occasionally come to light in compatibility assessments.

Eights are ambitious. They want to succeed and are well equipped to take advantage of almost any opportunity which comes their way. They are tough, practical and determined. They have the capacity for concentrated effort and will forge ahead with little support or encouragement. They can be hard, ruthless and obstinate in the pursuit of their goals and utterly unscrupulous in their methods. Unfortunately, Eight is the number of material failure as well as success. A combination of Eights will have to co-operate with each other if they don't want to turn a spectacular success into a spectacular failure.

The same Number Eight danger warning also holds true in career and family combinations. Learn how to give and take, don't go thinking you can always be the boss because you can't. You will have to share some of the glory and remember that you're up against one of your own number who can be just as mean and selfish.

Eight:Nine

This number combination often results in an excellent research team. Eight is practical and has stability while Nine draws his creative ideas from an entirely different thought plane. Eights and Nines can bring out the best in each other. Nine needn't worry about anything in the way of administration with an Eight for his partner, because Eights are responsible, self-disciplined and well-organized. They are tough, worldly-wise and very businesslike. They know exactly how to overcome obstacles and how to weather the odd storm that's sure to blow up from time to time.

All Nines need to do is add that inspirational touch to the whole operation and with their breadth of thought, mental supremacy and visionary outlook this should be a relatively simple task. They have clear, quick minds, great imaginations, high ideals and wide sympathies. But they must learn to take the odd word of criticism, avoid conceit and become less impulsive at times.

Average would be the best description for the Eight:Nine employment combinations. Eight Companies and individuals should always do well but when a Nine influence comes along it tends to detract from rather than enhance any potential because Nine is a strong, spiritual number which cancels out some of the Eight's materiality.

In the home Eight and Nine children will probably develop a healthy respect for each other because although Eights are usually aggressive and domineering they'll soon discover that they simply cannot push a Nine around. Nine is the highest of all the Love Number vibrations and the highly intelligent people ruled by it are quite capable of making their presence felt and their feelings known. This same mutual respect should also be present in the Eight:Nine and Nine:Eight parent/child relationships where no great problems are anticipated.

Nine:Nine

Wisdom, knowledge and a sincere desire to serve are just three of the special qualities to be found in this combination. A Nine:Nine partnership could do much to benefit humanity by sharing their own deep understanding of life with others. They are so well matched that they often form lifelong friendships but, unfortunately, they're not hard or aggressive enough to make a really resounding success of any joint business adventure they decide to embark upon.

Nines can be very strong-willed, determined characters particularly when they become passionately involved with some good cause or other or when they feel that their actions will ultimately benefit a great many people. Then they are resourceful, active, enterprising and courageous, prepared to fight for what they want and able to stir others into action with nothing more than their own enthusiasm.

However, they are also quick tempered and impulsive. At such times they need to choose their words with care or be prepared to suffer the consequences. Although two Nines don't really seem to have a great deal of business sense between them they are certainly not stupid and a Nine:Nine combination should be able to make some progress in a well-chosen commercial undertaking.

A Nine:Nine employee/employer combination can be excellent or mediocre; it all depends upon the company's outlook. If it happens to be concerned about people and cares what's happening in the world, then Nine will happily give his all for an organization which has high ideals. But if it only happens to manufacture washers or makes spare parts for helicopters he'll still work but not with that extra zeal and passion.

The Nine:Nine home front looks peaceful and harmonious for adult and child alike. People of this number rarely cause each other problems and the atmosphere should be one of happiness and contentment for Nine minds and bodies.

CHAPTER FIVE

Taking Numbers a Step Further

Now that you have discovered your Love Number and checked out your character, personality and relationship with other people, it is time to take numbers a step further and find your Life Number.

A Love Number is an extremely accurate portrait which relates to the personality with which you were born, but what you make of your innate potential is dictated by your Life Number. And this is mystically encoded within the letters of your name. Once you've unravelled the secret of your name, and it's not a difficult task, you can then achieve an even more accurate picture of yourself. A Love Number is a study in black and white and if you want to add colour, perspective and shading to the portrait you will need to know your Life Number.

To calculate this write out your name in capital letters then by referring to the following table:

1	2	3	4	5	6	7	8	9
A	B	C	D	E	F	G	H	I
J	K	L	M	N	O	P	Q	R
S	T	U	V	W	X	Y	Z	

write the corresponding numbers below each of the letters in your name. Here are two examples.

```
J O H N   S M I T H        M A R Y   B R O W N
1 6 8 5   1 4 9 2 8        4 1 9 7   2 9 6 5 5
```

You may wonder if you should include all your Christian names or, if you're a married/divorced woman, which surname you should use. The answer is surprisingly straightforward; the name you go by now is the name you should write down. If you never use all your Christian names, don't start now; if your surname is hyphenated write it all down and if you are normally known by a nickname, use that. What you are trying to find is the number which influences you at that particular moment in time so it really doesn't matter how many times you've changed your name in the past, how you choose to spell it, or anything else for that matter.

Add all the numbers together, one by one, from left to right. You should arrive at a two-figured number. Add these double digits together, a couple of times if necessary, until you're left with a single number from one to nine. This is your Life Number — make a note of it. Our two examples have been completed as shown.

$$J \quad O \quad H \quad N \quad S \quad M \quad I \quad T \quad H$$
$$1 + 6 + 8 + 5 \quad +1 + 4 + 9 + 2 + 8 = 44. \quad 4 + 4 = \text{Life}$$
$$\text{Number 8.}$$

$$M \quad A \quad R \quad Y \quad B \quad R \quad O \quad W \quad N$$
$$4 + 1 + 9 + 7 \quad +2 + 9 + 6 + 5 + 5 = 48. \quad 4 + 8 = 12. \ 1 + 2 =$$
$$\text{Life Number 3.}$$

Now you know your Life Number use the rest of this chapter for a full breakdown of each Love Number showing how the Life Numbers affect them. In this analysis, Love Numbers are shown first with the Life Numbers Second. For instance if your Love Number is Two and your Life Number is Six this would be shown as 2.6, or if Love is Eight and Life Nine, it will be 8.9.

Love/Life Combinations

One — The Leader

Positive traits: projective, powerful, dominating, pioneering.
Negative traits: obstinate, stubborn, dictatorial, impatient.

1.1 A double helping of One indicates great drive, energy, leadership and ambition but this person will need to keep his aggression in check if he doesn't want to make too many powerful enemies on his way to the top.

1.2   Two provides qualities which soften a One's natural aggression and give him or her the tact and diplomacy to put his plans into action in a friendly, amicable way. He should also find it easier to co-operate with others instead of trying to do everything by/for himself.

1.3   With the addition of charm and expertise contributed by the number Three, a One should find it easier to expand his ideas and turn them into real successes. Three gives him salesmanship. However, Three is a happy-go-lucky number while One is impulsive and concentration could be a real problem in this Love/Life combination.

1.4   One says go, Four says no. Between them a steadying influence is brought to bear. One is already full of ideas because he is innovative and original but the number Four gives him the staying power, practicality and thoroughness to see them through to their proper conclusion.

1.5   One may be full of bold, innovative ideas but he doesn't always know what best to do with them. That is where Five steps in to give him not only a large helping of versatility but also marketing skills and techniques. All One needs is a little publicity and Five shows him how to get it.

1.6   It's all very well to be pioneering and dynamic but everyone needs a little beauty and culture in their life or it would be very grim indeed. Six provides just the right amount here plus an extra little pinch of peace to make One less obstinate and impatient.

1.7   Seven provides balance because it brings spirituality to a worldly character and introversion to an extrovert. It also tends to slow One down because it makes him stop and think occasionally which is something he rarely has time for in his busy life.

1.8   A One with Eight tendencies is like a scorpion with two stings. One will become even more aggressive than he usually is, money will double in importance, speed will be of the essence and woe betide anyone who gets in his way.

1.9   Thank goodness for the number Nine because it brings wisdom, understanding and vision to a One. Once depth and breadth of thinking are added to his personality, someone with this combination of numbers should be less impulsive, and able to put his creativity to a more worthwhile use which could even benefit others less fortunate than himself.

TWO — The Sensitive

Positive traits: receptive submissive, persuasive conciliatory.
Negative traits: self-conscious, moody, indecisive, easily-influenced.

2.1   Twos are usually very shy and self-conscious but with an injection of One leadership, initiative and aggression they seem to achieve a more balanced outlook on life and are not quite so changeable and indecisive. One characteristics will also go a long way towards curing moodiness.

2.2   People with a strong Two influence tend to be afraid of their own shadows. Life seems to frighten them and they need a strong person to rely on and help them cope with all their insecurities. They can always see everyone else's point of view with the result that their own feelings and desires are never taken into account and they become resentful and bitter.

2.3   A Two never has any difficulty in making friends but with a Three influence he will know how to use these contacts to his advantage. With a greater helping of artistic talents and business acumen Two should be able to sell himself and his ideas much better.

2.4   The number Four always has a very comforting effect on a Two. It makes him more confident because he feels secure. And once he feels safe the positive side of his nature comes to the fore while his fears and self-consciousness pale into insignificance.

2.5   A very marked change comes over a Two when the Five influence is brought to bear on his life. He becomes bold and daring, full of life, sensual and game for anything. But unfortunately his moodiness often gets completely out of hand making him nervy and very unpredictable.

2.6   The number Six has a Venusian effect on a Two bringing with it peace of mind, balance and harmony. It is also a number connected with love and romance and should help Two get his changeable feelings and emotions into better perspective.

2.7   Seven always has a beneficial influence on a Two and while it may not actually make him more aggressive and dynamic it does give him a more philosophical outlook on life, and helps him come to terms with his shyness and lack of ambition. Unfortunately it also makes him more of a day-dreamer than he is already.

2.8 Eight is just the number Two needs to get him up on his feet and doing something positive with his life. He will be more ambitious, lively and energetic and much less hesitant and self-conscious. However, it certainly won't improve his emotional state because Eight is a number of great extremes.

2.9 Momentum is what a Two gains from the number Nine as well as insight, vision and above all hope. It is just what he needs to put him on the right track and the influence it has will make a marked, all-round improvement in both his personality and his attitude.

THREE — The Versatile

Positive traits: brilliant, imaginative, adaptable, lucky.
Negative traits: wasteful, frivolous, impulsive, outspoken.

3.1 A Three will often benefit greatly from a touch of One's fixity of purpose not to mention its courage, leadership and drive but what he must always guard against is allowing the spirit of adventure, which is associated with the number One, to lead him off in the wrong direction.

3.2 Threes are lively, brilliant and daring so a little modesty, tact and discretion certainly won't come amiss. Once they learn to take second place occasionally this will give them the opportunity to put their life into better order and give everyone else a chance to get a word in edgeways too.

3.3 An extra helping of 'Threeness' is the last thing that's needed here because a double dose of brilliance, imagination and versatility plus frivolity adds up to a very clever individual who never takes anything seriously and so wastes everyone's time including his own. However, a double Three could produce some highly original artwork.

3.4 Four is a useful number to combine with Three because it acts rather like a brake. Threes never really thinks things out carefully but Four will make them do this; Threes are very lively but Four will calm them down, and Three has some undeniably brilliant ideas and Four will provide the firm foundations to rest them on.

3.5 Five pushes Three's accelerator all the way down to the floor. There is always a feeling of 'live now — pay later' about this Love/Life combination. Both numbers generate ideas and Three provides the window-dressing while Five adds the marketing know-how. There are two very real dangers here — hastiness and over-production.

3.6 Once Six is added to Three the result is a more balanced outlook and a greater feeling of inner peace. Three's artistic talents should also be enhanced by a better appreciation of colour, beauty and design.

3.7 Energy, inspiration and ambition is what a Three has to offer so with the added benefit of Seven's ability to examine motives and tendencies and to deal productively with talents, Three should go from strength to strength.

3.8 Three has a positive genius for communicating ideas and packaging them attractively so with that extra surge of power and drive given by number Eight he can hardly fail to succeed. Eight can be a tricky number though, and if he doesn't take things seriously quite the reverse could happen.

3.9 A Three can be both spiritual and material in his outlook and with the addition of Nine he should take care to bring his idealism into focus and keep both feet firmly on the ground. Helping others is very commendable just as long as he always remembers to help himself first.

FOUR — The Builder

Positive traits: practical, steady, calm, respectable, efficient.
Negative traits: dull, suspicious, melancholic, contrary.

4.1 Fours are all solid, practical and well organized but what they lack is originality, creativity and aggression which One provides in just the right amount. Four could also find that with the addition of this number he is not quite so cautious and therefore he won't turn down so many opportunities even though they are a little on the speculative side.

4.2　Practicality and caution form the backbone of all Fours but add to this a touch of creativity, imagination and honour and you come up with a person who can bend a little more easily. Now add a further touch of finer feelings, tact and generosity and you have a flexible re-modelled Four.

4.3　Scope is what a number Three brings to a Four because it makes him more expansive and free-thinking. It makes him put his brain to creative use and he could come up with some interesting, viable ideas as a result.

4.4　A double Four can be so reliable, practical, down to earth and predictable that he makes you want to scream. He has no soul, no joy, no finer feelings and definitely no sense of humour. Safe as houses he may be but fun he most certainly is not.

4.5　Fours are balanced, practical and solid so a liberal helping of Five's daring, originality and impatience would be a distinct improvement especially if the undertones of Five's sexuality also creep into Four's private life.

4.6　There's no doubt about it, Fours are hard workers, whether for financial reward or the sheer hell of exerting themselves, so Six is the perfect number to bring a touch of beauty and imagination into their humdrum lives. Once they don their rose-coloured Six spectacles the world will seem a far nicer place.

4.7　Anyone with a Love/Life combination of 4.7 could achieve great things because Four gives them strength, practicality and thoroughness leaving Seven free to add insight and imagination. Put all these talents and characteristics together in one person and almost perfect balance is achieved.

4.8　A Four with Eight overtones has the best of both worlds because he can see everything on two different scales, the small scale which he gets from his Love Number and the large scale which comes with the number Eight. Eight also provides creative energy which sweeps away innate caution and then a Four becomes virtually unstoppable.

4.9　Four is practical and functions on the material, earthly plane but when Nine comes along bringing higher values and philosophies the change in Four is really quite astounding. Once armed with reason, judgement, wisdom and insight, he seems to rise above himself and gains a broader overall picture of life.

FIVE — The Adventurer

Positive traits: clever, resourceful, resilient, original, sexual.
Negative traits: restless, quick-tempered, highly-strung, lustful.

5.1   Fives can definitely do with a generous helping of One single-mindedness to keep them heading in the same direction for more than five minutes at a time. They could also benefit from more ambition although obstinacy and selfishness are two extra negative One traits they could do without because they have more than enough of their own already.

5.2   The cold water treatment that Two would undoubtedly give a Five could be a very good thing because it would certainly cool him down a bit and that's exactly what a fidgety, restless Five needs. Some Two shyness and modesty might also curb his rampant sexuality slightly.

5.3   There's always a very real danger when Three exerts its influence on a Five that matters will get completely out of hand. Fives are quite clever enough without a second helping of brilliance, daring and charm. They can never be pinned down at the best of times and when Three, which is an easy-going number, is added you will never get a straight answer out of them.

5.4   The Four vibration does wonders for an adventurous Five because it makes him more cautious and reliable. Four is solid, practical and organized and nobody needs these extra qualities more than a jumpy, restless Five. This Life Number influence is good.

5.5   Two Fives are without a doubt the worst possible combination of Love/Life Numbers. All Fives are restless and dislike being tied down so, when doubly influenced by this number, the individuals concerned are liable to be temperamental, highly excitable and perhaps even slightly unstable. The only thing they have going for them is the fact that they are resilient, so let's hope they recover quickly from all the problems they are fated to encounter along life's path.

5.6 A combination like this is potentially good because Six brings peace and harmony to the fidgety Five. It also lends form and beauty to his ideas and because Six is concerned with mother love it effectively tones down the Five's insatiable sexuality.

5.7 Seven is the magic number and it certainly casts a spell over Five because once under its calming influence he can occasionally be found reading a book, writing letters or just quietly relaxing. This sort of behaviour is most out of character but not to be discouraged.

5.8 The number Eight acts as a rocket booster on an already vivacious Five and it's to be hoped that he knows where he's going before he blasts off into orbit. Dynamic is hardly a strong enough word for a 5.8 and he could be heading for trouble unless he gets some proper direction in his life — and fast.

5.9 An energetic Five with the wisdom, vision and sagacity of a Nine could go a very long way indeed although there is one enormous stumbling block in his path. Five is impulsive at the best of times and when this major Nine fault gives him a second helping of this undesirable trait he will need to learn tremendous self-control if he wants to make his fabulous journey all in one piece.

SIX — The Peacemaker

Positive traits: beauty, harmony, love, creativity, domesticity, fidelity.
Negative traits: conventionality, forcefulness, complacency, triviality.

6.1 Quiet, peaceful Sixes can sometimes do with a shake-up to stop them becoming too complacent and the number One makes them rather more aggressive than they are normally inclined to be. It also makes them more projective while at the same time doubling their sense of responsibility for their loved ones.

6.2 Sixes are always glad to receive an extra helping of pleasant qualities so when Two offers them extra creativity, artistic flair and imagination they willingly accept. Unfortunately this is a package deal and Two's moodiness and jealousy can be very disruptive for a normally well-balanced Six to come to terms with.

6.3   Domesticated Sixes of both sexes love to socialize and entertain their friends and with a strong Three influence this tends to make them more congenial and charming than ever. However, Three is a wasteful, frivolous number and a Six who doesn't take thrift and economy seriously is a real contradiction in terms.

6.4   Four can be a rather dull, joyless number at times and when coupled with a Six it does tend to clip the creative wings quite savagely. However, by way of compensation, it doubly endorses the homeloving instincts of a 6.4 person despite the fact that it does nothing for the spiritual side of their nature.

6.5   An impatient Five influence unsettles a Six because a wicked little voice keeps whispering in his ear, tempting him to do something a bit more exciting and adventurous. The Five vibration often causes him identity problems and sometimes he never appears to know whether he's coming or going.

6.6   This combination of Love/Life Numbers can be rather nauseous as too much sweetness and light isn't always a good thing. Anyone influenced by the double Six should be able to create an atmosphere of incredible beauty and should also be exceptionally artistically talented.

6.7   A seven influence effectively turns a Six into a split personality because the Six half of him remains involved in domestic, creative and artistic endeavours while the Seven part wants to be left alone to explore the mind through meditation. It always takes a tremendous effort for Six to achieve anything like balance when he's being pulled in two different directions at once.

6.8   Eight effectively provides Six with the business sense he has always lacked and as long as the Eight influence doesn't become too dominant this can be a very good thing. With stronger financial and commercial tendencies Six should be able to promote the sale of his work far better than usual.

6.9   Beauty (six) and truth (nine) is what a 6.9 Love/Life Number combination is all about. With the addition of Nine vision, resourcefulness and intuition Six can only benefit from this liaison, although he may decide to reject Nine's impulsiveness and hasty temper.

SEVEN — The Mysterious

Positive traits: mystical, intellectual, philosophical, self-controlled.
Negative traits: confusing, aloof, secretive, doubting.

7.1 Sevens are magical, mysterious and very unworldly so a good dose of One characteristics is the best medicine to bring them down to earth with a realistic thump. Add to that some One determination, ambition and aggression and Seven, with all his creative ideas, immediately becomes a much more viable proposition all round.

7.2 Under the secondary influence of Two, Seven becomes even more calm and serene than he usually is, as well as changeable, hesitant and terribly indecisive. He also undergoes marked emotional changes which are not particularly desirable as they make him very suspicious and possessive about the object of his affections.

7.3 Seven has understanding and deep insight which he usually prefers to keep to himself but once influenced by the number Three he comes right out of his shell and turns into a very sociable fellow indeed. He also gains greater drive but unfortunately his concentration suffers under this vibration and he isn't able to think quite so clearly.

7.4 What could be better than a Four influence to keep Seven in daily touch with reality? He usually lives in a little world of his own on an entirely different level of consciousness to everyone else but the number Four will make him not only more realistic but more practical, stable and better organized too.

7.5 Travel is the keyword here as both numbers are associated with it. A Seven normally goes in search of truth but with the addition of Five he could have some very strange, exciting adventures along the way. The number Five should make him a livelier person all round and it's anyone's guess how the extra sexuality it generates will affect him.

7.6 The Six influence should broaden Seven's horizons of thought. Instead of just concerning himself with philosophy, religion, life's mysteries and the occult, he'll be able to add art, poetry, design and music to his list. Six will also make him more homely and better equipped to deal with his personal needs, in other words — more domesticated.

7.7   That extra Seven is one too many because people who are heavily influenced by this number are in great danger of rejecting the physical world altogether, preferring to live in a world of ideas which exists only in their imagination. These sort of people are reclusive and tend to hide from reality in complete isolation.

7.8   A Seven has insight, imagination and vision and the wicked number Eight, which can swing from one extreme to the other, will either set him on fire with enthusiasm or burn him to a cinder. Eight is a number of strength and force and a Seven with Eight overtones could do very nicely for himself provided he gets himself sufficiently motivated.

7.9   Greater wisdom, understanding and perfect peace are all estimable qualities which Nine will definitely give to Seven but what he really needs is more get up and go which Nine doesn't provide. Impulsiveness will definitely rub off on him so when he does decide to make a move let's hope it isn't on the spur of the moment or in entirely the wrong direction.

EIGHT — The Materialist

Positive traits: tough, strong, practical, tenacious, ambitious.
Negative traits: aggressive, ruthless, unscrupulous, tyrannical, selfish.

8.1   Heaven help anyone who stands in the way of someone influenced by this 8.1 Love/Life Number combination because they'll be lucky to escape with their life. These two numbers create a powerhouse of forceful, aggressive energy which will never rest until complete, utter, total and ultimate success has been achieved.

8.2   Diplomacy and tact are what Two brings to Eight and a meeker, quieter, watered-down Eight could be a distinct improvement. The moodiness and jealousy which are associated with Two could play havoc with Eight because he's already reached saturation point all by himself with both these undesirable traits without the addition of any more.

8.3   Eight can always do with a good PR/advertising agent and under the Three vibration he can have these skills ready-made and built in free of charge. The Three influence will also make him more socially in demand because it adds wit, charm and vivacity to his innate wisdom and strength.

8.4   An Eight will embrace Four characteristics warmly because they are extremely useful to him. He tends to see everything on a grand, overall scale but when Four is added he will be able to see the small details. Once he has the ability to spot all the tiny flaws in his schemes he will be able to put minor errors right before they do any great, irreparable damage to his master plans.

8.5   Greased lightning is what this combination is like because with a generous helping of Five nervous energy Eight can be there and back again before anyone has even noticed, which can be a distinct advantage in some of the power games that Eights love to play. And a good, honest helping of Five sensuality should also cure the majority of his emotional hang-ups.

8.6   Mercenary and materialistic is what Eights are and they often have no values in life other than purely monetary ones. But when Six is added Eight suddenly becomes aware of the finer things like beauty and art, gains inner peace and gentleness and becomes generally a far nicer, less aggressive person altogether.

8.7   Tremendous calm and tranquility sweeps over Eight under a Seven spell with the result that money, power and success become much less important to him. He seems to spend far more time deeply engrossed in thought and even his outlook changes from purely materialistic to strangely philosophical.

8.8   If you ever want to start a revolution look for someone with this combination of numbers to lead it for you, then sit back and wait for the trouble to start. Raw energy is what we're dealing with here and it needs to be handled with great respect because it is very unstable and could blow up in someone's face at any moment.

8.9   Spirituality is what Nine brings to Eight, along with a sense of balance because it neutralizes his materialism. With his innate strength and practicality and a touch of Nine creativity and vision an 8.9 should go far without upsetting anyone in the process.

NINE — The Visionary

Positive traits: large-minded, idealistic, humanitarian, courageous.
Negative traits: intolerant, obstinate, impulsive, quick-tempered.

9.1   The originality and dash which One injects here could turn an ordinary Nine, if any Nine could ever be described as such, into an inventive genius. However, an extra helping of obstinacy and aggression will mean that Nine will need to watch his hasty temper and learn to control it better.

9.2   A Nine with Two tact, discretion and powers of persuasion, not to mention the ability to see both sides of an argument, should be in a strong position to get his humanitarian schemes passed and implemented. However, a Nine with Two shyness and hesitancy won't get anywhere very quickly.

9.3   Nines often get so wrapped up in their struggle to save mankind from nuclear attack, poverty and starvation that they often forget to take time off to enjoy themselves. But when the number Three influences them the balance is restored and they become more easy-going and much less intense. Good luck also seems to come their way as an added Three bonus.

9.4   Four is a solid, practical, down-to-earth number and a little 'Fourness' should soon square up a spiritual, visionary Nine. Many of his plans are rejected because they are unrealistic or impractical so a little Four common sense would also be a good thing.

9.5   The number Five is like a two-edged sword when it comes into contact with Nine because it carried benefits and drawbacks so it can cut both ways. Nine could do with some Five versatility, originality and brilliance but the last thing he needs is increased impulsion — he has a surfeit of that already.

9.6   All Nines are visionary and large-minded. They see the effects of everything on a universal (macrocosmic) scale. Then along comes the number Six concerned with domesticity and the family (microcosmic) unit and Nine immediately gains more detailed understanding. So what Six effectively does is to make a Nine see the importance of the smaller scale as well as the larger scale of humanity.

9.7 Seven brings 'inner growth' to a Nine as well as self-control, clairvoyance to go with his vision, and even greater imagination. The Seven influence will also make Nine stop and think a little more often before he acts or speaks and this is perhaps the greatest benefit of all.

9.8 Nine is very spiritual and idealistic so a good helping of Eight materialism, practicality and ambition should benefit him enormously. He could do with more common sense and a down-to-earth attitude towards not only money but life in general too because sometimes he's far too high-minded for his own god.

9.9 We already know that Nine is the highest Love Number vibration of all so when Nine is also the Life Number this indicates a person of overwhelming spiritual and mental supremacy, perhaps even a genius. However, there's only a fine dividing line between brilliance and insanity and anyone ruled by this particular combination should always remember this.

CHAPTER SIX

Compatibility Charts

There are four rules of thumb you need to remember when you establish compatibility ratings between people and their Love Numbers, but these points are only intended as guides and certainly don't constitute hard and fast numerological rules; they are given simply to help you with your own attempts at analysis and do not have to be rigidly observed.

First, remember that all numbers, whether odd or even, have negative as well as positive characteristics, and odd numbers (1, 3, 5, 7 and 9) are generally masculine, active, creative and extrovert while even numbers (2, 4, 6 and 8) are generally feminine, passive, receptive and introvert.

Secondly, are the two numbers that you're concerned with both odd or even? If the answer is 'yes', then such a combination indicates harmonious coexistence because both partners will have special qualities of their own (which the other lacks) to contribute to the relationship with the result that they tend to bring out the best, rather than the worst, in each other. But if the answer to the question is 'no' then we arrive at the third point to watch out for, which occurs when two numbers being analysed oppose each other — one odd, one even. In numerology they are called 'Conflicting Numbers' and when such a combination exists there are often very marked differences of opinion and frequent clashes of personality between the people in question. They can still be physically attracted but their difficulty lies in a true understanding of one another. A great deal of mutual give and take is needed to make such a partnership work.

Love Numbers can also be divided into three separate groups. One, Five and Seven are all 'Mind' numbers and people ruled by them are often intellectual, well-educated and great thinkers. The next group, which houses the 'Expression' numbers Three, Six and Nine indicates emotional, creative and, at times, inspired individuals. Many writers and artists fall into this cateogry. Finally people whose birthdate reduces to one of the 'Business' numbers, Two, Four and Eight, are good organizers. They are stable, efficient and business-minded. In fact many of them become merchants, bankers and executives. So the final question to ask yourself is whether the two numbers you're looking at come from the same numerical group or not. If they do the combination should be fairly compatible because it indicates two people of similar ability and temperament.

Let's now look at the compatibility charts, which detail every possible combination of Love Numbers. Ratings are given for all types of relationship from the very personal right through to business and family combinations. They can be used as a quick-glance guide or a check for your own compatibility findings. The grades given are as follows:

A = Excellent/almost perfect

B = Good

C = Average

D = Poor

E = Disastrous

You will notice that some of the combinations have been given two ratings, for example, 'A/E' where a Love Number Eight is paired with another Love Number Eight or 'B/D' where a Love Number Three is linked with a Love Number Five and so on. These double ratings quite simply indicate the extremes the relationship in question could reach.

Combination	Personal Male/Female Relationship	Personal Female/Male Relationship	Business Partnership	Employee/ Employer	Employer/ Employee	Child/ Child	Parent/ Child
1:1	B	B	A/E	A/B	A/B	E	B/D
1:2	B/C	C	B/C	B	C	B	C
1:3	B	A/B	B/D	C	B	C	B
1:4	C/D	D	D	D	D	D	D
1:5	C/E	B/E	C	B/C	C	C	C/D
1:6	C	B/C	B/C	B/C	B/C	B/C	B/C
1:7	B/C	B/D	D	C/D	D	C	C/D
1:8	A/E	A/E	A/E	A/E	A/E	A/E	B/D
1:9	A/C	B/C	B	B	B	B	B/C
2:1	C	B/C	B/C	C	B	B	C
2:2	A	A	D/E	D/E	D/E	A/B	A/B
2:3	C/E	C	B/C	A/B	A/B	B	C
2:4	B	B	B/C	B/C	B/C	A/B	A/B
2:5	D	D/E	D/E	D	D/E	C/E	C/D
2:6	B	A/B	D	C	C	A/B	A/B
2:7	B/C	B	D/E	C	C/D	B	B
2:8	C/D	C	B/C	B/C	C	B/C	C
2:9	B/C	B/C	A/B	A/B	A/B	A/B	A/B

Combination	Personal Male/Female Relationship	Personal Female/Male Relationship	Business Partnership	Employee/Employer	Employer/Employee	Child/Child	Parent/Child
3:1	A/B	B	B/D	B	C	C	B
3:2	C	C/E	B/C	A/B	A/B	B	B
3:3	D	D	E	E	E	A/C	A/C
3:4	C	C/D	B/D	C	C	D	C/D
3:5	B/D	C	B/C	B/E	B/E	B/E	C
3:6	B	B/C	B/C	B	C	B	A/C
3:7	C	C	B	B	C/D	C	B
3:8	B/D	B/D	A/B	A/B	A/B	A/B	C
3:9	A	C/D	D/E	C	B/C	B	B
4:1	D	C/D	D	D	D	D	D
4:2	B	B	B/C	B/C	B/C	A/B	A/B
4:3	C/D	C	B/D	C	C	D	C/D
4:4	A	A	A	A	A	A	A
4:5	C	C	B/C	D/E	D/E	D	D
4:6	B/C	C	B	A/B	A/B	A/B	A/B
4:7	C	B/C	B	A/B	C	C/D	C/D
4:8	A/B	A/B	A	B	A	A	A
4:9	B/C	C	D	C	C	C	B/C

Combination	Personal Male/Female Relationship	Personal Female/Male Relationship	Business Partnership	Employee/ Employer	Employer/ Employee	Child/ Child	Parent/ Child
5:1	B/E	C/E	C	C	B/C	C	C
5:2	D/E	D	D/E	D/E	D	C/E	C/D
5:3	C	B/D	B/C	B/E	B/E	B/E	C
5:4	C	C	B/C	D/E	D/E	D	D
5:5	E	E	E	E	E	E	E
5:6	A/B	B/C	C/D	C/D	C/D	C	D
5:7	B/D	D/E	D/E	E	E	D/E	D
5:8	B/C	C/E	A/D	A/B	B	B/D	D/E
5:9	C	C/E	C	D	D	C	B/C
6:1	B/C	C	B/C	B/C	B/C	B/C	C/D
6:2	A/B	B	D	C	C	A/B	B/C
6:3	B/C	B	B/C	C	C	A	A/B
6:4	C	B/C	B	A/B	A/B	A/B	A/C
6:5	B/C	A/B	C/D	C/D	C/D	C	A/B
6:6	A	A	C/D	C	C	A	D
6:7	D/E	C	E	E	E	E	A
6:8	B/C	C	A/B	A/B	A/B	C	E
6:9	A/B	A/B	C/D	D	D	A	C

Combination	Personal Male/Female Relationship	Personal Female/Male Relationship	Business Partnership	Employee/ Employer	Employer/ Employee	Child/ Child	Parent/ Child
7:1	B/D	B/C	D	D	C/D	C	C/D
7:2	B	B/C	D/E	C/D	C	B	B
7:3	C	C	B	B	C/D	C	C
7:4	B/C	C	B	C	A/B	C/D	C/D
7:5	D/E	B/D	D/E	E	E	D/E	D/E
7:6	C	D/E	E	E	E	E	E
7:7	A	A	E	D/E	D/E	A	A
7:8	B/C	B/D	C	C/D	C	C/D	D
7:9	A	A	D	D	D	A/B	A/B
8:1	A/E	A/E	A/E	A/E	A/E	A/E	B/D
8:2	C	C/D	B/C	C	B/C	B/C	B/C
8:3	B/D	B/D	A/B	A/B	A/B	A/B	A/B
8:4	A/B	A/B	A	A	B	A	A
8:5	C/E	B/C	A/D	B	A/B	B/D	B
8:6	C	B/C	A/B	A/B	A/B	C	C/D
8:7	B/D	B/C	C	C	C/D	C/D	D
8:8	A/E	A/E	A/E	A/E	A/E	A/E	A/E
8:9	C	E	B/C	C	C	C	C

Combination	Personal Male/Female Relationship	Personal Female/Male Relationship	Business Partnership	Employee/ Employer	Employer/ Employee	Child/ Child	Parent/ Child
9:1	B/C	A/C	B	B	B	B	B/C
9:2	B/C	B/C	A/B	A/B	A/B	A/B	A/B
9:3	C/D	A	D/E	B/C	C	B	B
9:4	C	B/C	D	C	C	C	C
9:5	C/E	C	C	D	D	C	C/D
9:6	A/B	A/B	C/D	D	D	A	A
9:7	A/B	A	D	D	D	A/B	A/B
9:8	E	C	B/C	C	C	C	C
9:9	A	A	C/D	A/D	A/D	A	A

Of further interest . . .

FORTUNE-TELLING
BY DICE

Uncovering the Future Through
the Ancient System of
Casting Lots

FORTUNE-TELLING BY DICE

David and Julia Line. In the *only* book of its kind available David and
Julia Line explain a complete system of fortune-telling, requiring only
three dice of different colours (red, green and white). Over 650 individual
meanings are given for dice thrown in groups of three in an extensive
reference section, and every possible combination is covered by the 3
categories — 'General Situation', 'Finance/Business', 'Love/Affection'. With
a series of casebook studies they trace the background to this method
of fortune-telling and illustrate the accuracy of dice in the divination
scene.

FORTUNE TELLING BY RUNES
A GUIDE TO CASTING AND INTERPRETING
THE ANCIENT EUROPEAN RUNE STONES

David and Julia Line. Casting runes to shed light on the future is one of the least well documented methods of divination, and yet it is one of the easiest, and is remarkable in its accuracy. Here is an essentially practical book, containing all the information needed to cast rune stones and to interpret individual and group meanings from where the stones fall on a runic chart. The authors demonstrate the simplicity of the techniques involved and show that anyone can learn to use the runes to discover the secret of what their future holds.

Numerology:
The Power
to Know
Anybody

Use the hidden power
of numbers to achieve
startling and valuable
results in your life.

D. Jason Cooper

Learn how to:
- construct your own numeroscope
- analyse your name number
- determine your destiny number
- succeed through numerology

NUMEROLOGY: THE POWER TO KNOW ANYONE

D. J. Cooper. The most *precise* science is the science of numbers. For hundreds of years men has sought to apply this precision to the forces which daily shape our lives and therefore our futures. Much has been written on the subject using the Pythagorean system but **D. Jason Cooper** here uses Ulian numerology for specific *character* insights rather than general analysis. Simple to use yet fascinating in application, this is a book that anyone, even those with no previous experience, can use successfully.

THE
NUMEROLOGY
WORKBOOK
Understanding and Using the Power of Numbers

3

JULIA LINE

THE NUMEROLOGY WORKBOOK

Julia Line. *What is your personal number and what does it reveal about you? What is the secret number of the Bible? How are 'The Abyss', the Rig Veda, Jesus and Mary, and pure silver linked?* In this — undoubtedly the most exciting numerology workbook ever produced — **Julia Line** answers these questions, explains what numerology IS, and shows how YOU can use it to:

- Reveal your true spiritual nature
- Discover your years of 'peak' potential
- Use colours and music to mystically harmonize your life
- Find your perfect mate
- Uncover hidden talents and reveal your ideal career
- Predict the future and expose your destiny
- Understand the numerical meaning of the Tarot

Easy to use yet amazingly comprehensive, this fascinating book allows YOU to develop your own style from the most popular systems of numerology including Pythagorean, Golden Dawn and Cheiro. *Solve the enigmas of existence with THE NUMEROLOGY WORKBOOK by Julia Line.*